Child Domestic Workers
in Zimbabwe

Child Domestic Workers in Zimbabwe

by
Michael Bourdillon,
with Tinashe Pfigu, Jeremiah Chinodya,
Rumbidzai Rurevo, and many working children

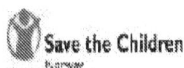

Save the Children
Norway

WEAVER
W
—PRESS—

Published by Weaver Press, Box A1922, Avondale, Harare. 2006

Typeset by Weaver Press
Cover Design: Xealos
Cover Photograph: Weaver Press
Printed by: Sable Press, Harare.

The author and the publishers would like to express their
gratitude to Save the Children (Norway) for their support in the
research and production of this book.

ISBN: 1 77922 044 8

Acknowledgments

Many people have contributed time and effort in providing the material we have used for this book. Most of all, we acknowledge our debt to the children, many of whom gave time in the midst of heavy workloads. We hope that the publication of the stories of some children will help many of them.

We also acknowledge co-operation from employers who have allowed children in their charge to attend meetings and to talk to us, and who have sometimes given of their own time to discuss issues. This applies especially to the employers of three children who allowed us to intrude into their homes.

The following officers of the Zimbabwe Domestic and Allied Workers' Union have worked well with the children, given their time to various workshops and discussions, and accompanied field researchers: Helarious Ruyi, Percival Goremusandu, Cuthbert Mambudzi, Mr Chikwenya, MrHuni, Ketso Mahabo, Wellington Chiparamakura, Florence Mudzengerere, Mr Shikozho, and Fanwell Chayamano.

The research and the production of this book depended on the support of the Zimbabwe office of Save the Children, Norway, especially of Lois Mushonga and Caroline Chikowore.

I am particularly grateful to the African Studies Centre, Leiden, The Netherlands, for a visiting fellowship in 2005, which enabled me to complete the writing and widen my background reading.

Michael Bourdillon
October 2005

Table of Contents

Foreword

Child domestic work has given rise to controversy throughout the world. Many people justify employing children to look after the house as a way of providing an income for poor children and their families. In our situation in Zimbabwe, it is sometimes a route to providing orphans with a means of livelihood. Some children use their labour to fund the expenses necessary to complete their schooling.

Others condemn child domestic work as one of the worst forms of child labour. Child domestic workers are often humiliated and abused, verbally and physically. They often work long hours, with no time when they are formally off duty. They are prevented from completing their education, or from leaving the home of the employer, because they are physically locked into the house. In addition, the pay is often very low as employers want to ensure that they do not have the means to return to their own homes. As a result, their self-esteem is low and their development is impaired.

Professor Michael Bourdillon's study shows both sides of this argument. This work shows that some children see their position in domestic employment as helpful, even to the extent of taking pride in how they have used such a position to see themselves through difficult times. On the other hand, many of the children are working under duress. They are unhappy in their work, and particularly with the lack of respect shown to them by employers and their families.

Children are our future. If someone wants to help a child from a poor family by employing him or her to do tasks in the home, they need to ensure that the child is able to develop – physically, socially, intellectually, and psychologically.

In light of the foregoing, Save the Children Norway-Zimbabwe supported the work of the Zimbabwe Domestic and Allied Workers Union and the research process spearheaded by Professor Bourdillon because of our passion and commitment to Zimbabwe's children. It is imperative for SCN to support work for and with children as this forms the core of our values.

This book points to areas to which those who employ children need to pay particular attention. It also serves to remind us of our responsibilities to the young in our society, and especially to those children who suffer harsh treatment, so compounding the traumas they have already experienced in their troubled lives.

Lois Mushonga
Country Director: Save the Children (Norway)
Zimbabwe, 2005

1

Introduction

Many children in Zimbabwe help to support themselves and their families by working for an income. In the face of growing poverty and the deaths of many adults from HIV/AIDS, children cannot always depend on the adult world for support. Indeed, they often take pride in their contributions to their own upkeep and that of their families.[1] This booklet is mainly about children who support themselves through domestic employment, although it also says something on domestic work by children in their own homes. While the information presented here has been gathered mainly from children in the urban areas, the problem of child domestic employment also exists in the rural areas.[2]

In writing this book, we have avoided the term 'child labour', which generally raises strong reactions of horror at the thought of children toiling long hours in bad conditions for low pay. Child work and child employment are not always like this. We, the authors, are not trying to prevent the employment of child domestic workers in situations where employers care for the children who work for them and take their well-being seriously. But we wish to alert employers to some of the difficulties that the children face. Although some of the children we met appear to be content in their domestic employment, many are unhappy for a variety of reasons and are working under duress. These children need our attention and support. Another purpose of this book is to alert people generally to the way in which child domestic workers are sometimes degraded and abused.

In most societies, children are not supposed to be idle. They have schoolwork to do at school and at home (and even this can sometimes be excessive and amount to abuse). It is part of the culture in Zimbabwe, as in many societies throughout the world, that children have to help with household chores – children in rural areas are expected to help run the family farm and look after livestock. Indeed in the 1980s, supported by the idea of African Socialism, Zimbabwe adopted a policy of combining education with productive work, as did many other African societies.[3] We are not opposed to children working.

We are not opposed to children being paid for the work they do. Within the family, it is usual for children to work as part of their responsibility to the family in which they are living. In return, they receive family resources. If they perform similar work for other people, they do not benefit in the same way from the resources of the home and so it is appropriate for them to benefit in other ways.

Whether children are in their own home, or earning their keep with kin, or working for others, we are concerned about the amount of work, and the kinds of work they are required to do. We are concerned that their education should continue to useful levels. We are concerned that their health is not impaired in any way. We are concerned that they be treated with respect and dignity. We are concerned that they have a chance to enjoy themselves and to socialise with their peers. We are concerned about responsibility placed on children who are not mature enough to take it on. We are concerned about the conditions of their life and work.

The policy of the Save the Children Alliance is that not all work is harmful to children, and that we need to distinguish the positive and negative effects of children's work.[4] A key tool in helping us to decide when work is so harmful as to require the urgent removal of children from the situation, is Convention 182 on the worst forms of child labour, passed by the International Labour Organisation (ILO) in 1999 and since ratified by most countries in the world. Two of the criteria of the worst forms of child labour may apply to domestic work in specific situations.

One criterion is that domestic work may involve forced or compulsory labour:[5] children are sometimes forced to work by parents, guardians or employers, and are sometimes prevented from leaving their work by employers. This is exacerbated when the children are removed far from their family home in order to work, bringing an element of child trafficking into their employment situation.

Second, work can be classified as one of the worst forms of child labour when by its nature or by the circumstances in which it is carried out, it is likely to harm the health, safety, or morals of children.[6] Excessive hours, lack of sleep, unsafe practices, and various forms of psychological, physical, or sexual abuse, can bring domestic work into this category. Working in isolation or at night may also be harmful to the child.[7]

In many parts of the world, child domestic workers are frequently subject to these kinds of abuse. In particular, they suffer low self esteem, and find themselves growing up alienated from social life.[8] Some people argue that the situation of child domestic workers is so bad that this should be considered one of the worst forms of child labour, to be eliminated entirely.[9] While this may be true in some countries, our study indicates that in Zimbabwe, some children benefit from employment in domestic service and that their lives would be damaged more if their employment were banned. Nevertheless, many children do suffer in domestic employment. In particular, they are frequently insulted, which can be damaging to a child's esteem..

One aim of the study behind this book was to explore the extent of the worst forms of child labour in child domestic work in Zimbabwe. This could not easily be assessed directly. Child domestic work is often hidden, taking place in private homes and further concealed by attributing kinship relationships between the employers and the children. Moreover, employers who treat children particularly badly do not readily allow outsiders to investigate the situations of these children.

To collect information, we approached child domestic workers with whom we already had contact through clubs facilitated by officers of the Zimbabwe Domestic and Allied Workers' Union (ZDAWU) to find out how they view their work, and about the problems they face. The problems of some of them were severe, and they were able to tell us of other children they knew who were in even worse situations. So while we do not have statistics or figures, we have an idea of the serious problems facing some child domestic workers and that need urgent redress.

While many child domestic workers are treated badly, others are happy in their situations and derive benefits from their work. Others still do not wish to lose their opportunity for improving their situation through employment, but they are not happy with their conditions of work. This study allows the children to air their complaints about the way they are treated, and to find ways of improving their situation. Even those employers who are kind and considerate to the children they employ, need to think carefully about the children's needs.

Whilst the worst cases of abuse require urgent attention, we should not be complacent about the situation of other child domestic workers, who frequently suffer loneliness and unhappiness and who have little opportunity to complain, or to bargain to improve their position. Child domestic work is by its very nature problematic, since it places children in a low social position while they are growing up. If we focus only on severe cases of abuse, we will appear to condone the other ways in which child domestic workers suffer.[10]

When children are employed in domestic service in return for their keep, they are given chores similar to those performed by children in any household. Their situation is frequently viewed in the light of traditions according to which children are often brought up outside their parental home, to learn social skills and responsibilities.[11] In particular, the relationships of children with their grandparents, as well as with certain uncles and aunts, are less authoritarian than their relationships with parents, thus enabling freer discussion and the passing of information about sensitive topics like sex. Accordingly children may live with kin for years at a time, performing household chores in exchange for support and training. Unfortunately, such family traditions do not always protect children from harm, especially when they are adopted in altered circumstances, such as in a monetary economy in an urban area, away from the controls and support of the child's immediate family.

Children work in domestic service in a wide variety of situations. We find children working for kin, sometimes for no pay. We find children being employed by friends of the family or by strangers to them. We find children employed to do odd or occasional domestic chores, as well as children who are full-time, live-in domestic servants. We find child domestic workers in rural households, in high-density city suburbs, as well as in spacious homes in the wealthier parts of towns and cities. Numbers are hard to assess since many of the workers themselves disguise their position for fear of interference: we estimate very roughly that there are over 30,000 children employed as domestic workers in the urban areas of Zimbabwe.[12]

In child domestic work, it is not always easy to separate the positive and negative effects of work. Exploitative employment is often combined with patronage, in which the employer is helping a poorer child. Sometimes it is not possible to disentangle the benefit that the child receives, from the exploitation of a disadvantaged child by a more powerful employer. On the one hand, a wealthy family provides a home and support for a poorer child; many of the children are happy in their work and in their place of employment, and wish for no interference. On the other hand, the children supply cheap and pliant labour for the wealthier household. It is easy for adults to exploit these children, either through deliberate intent to get the most out of them, or through inattention to the children's needs.. The children are in a vulnerable position, and rarely do they have the power to negotiate improvements to their terms of employment. It is tempting to take advantage of those who are unable to defend themselves. Many of the children are unhappy with their situation and want it to be improved. Some are very unhappy, beaten and abused, on call all day and every day for small rewards and these deserve our urgent attention and protection. When we come across employers treating children badly, to be silent is to be complicit in the crime.

The most common complaint of the children is that they are treated without respect, insulted, shouted at, even beaten, and treated as if they have no thoughts or feelings. When children are learning to cope with difficulties, such as perhaps with the loss of parents, by earning their keep through conscientious work, they deserve respect and appreciation, not further trauma through insulting and degrading treatment.

Two factors inhibit respect for working children. One is the stereotypical assumption that children are ignorant and incompetent (which we shall be discussing shortly). The second relates to class. Working children come from poor backgrounds and usually work for relatively wealthy families. In a society in which status is often assessed in relation to material wealth, it is easy to despise those without such signs of status. People without resources are powerless and readily manipulated. A class structure that treats the poor with contempt fuels the lack of respect for working children.

Child domestic workers are entrusted to take care of the home and usually at times to look after the younger children of the household. Without the respect and rewards that these responsibilities deserve, children are unlikely to be content in their work and they are unlikely to perform well. Besides, to be treated with respect and dignity is a fundamental human right.

Children's Rights

People sometimes think of the concern for human rights, and the rights of children in particular, as a peculiarly western concern, not necessarily in keeping with African culture. Such people argue that it is more important to pay attention to our own culture and make sure children are brought up to know how to behave in our society. Talk about the rights of children is less important than training children how to behave within their own culture.

The need for international agreement on human rights became particularly apparent after the atrocities of the Second World War and in particular, the atrocities of the Nazis against the Jews. People agreed that there are certain things that are not acceptable in the way we treat other peoples and that such things cannot be justified on the grounds of national laws and national sovereignty. The reason for discussing rights is to agree on fundamental principles that are more important than national governments or local cultures.

Although there has been long-standing discussion on children's rights, focus on these in international conventions is recent. The driving force behind formulating children's rights in the United Nations Convention for the Rights of the Child (1989 – CRC) came from European countries. The formulation of the rights, however, involved input from people from around the world and all but two countries in the world (one of the exceptions being the United States of America) have ratified the convention, indicating their agreement to its principles. Shortly after this, in 1990, the Organisation of African Unity adopted the African Charter on the Rights and Welfare of the Child (AC), which closely follows the CRC. The rights spoken of in these conventions have therefore been widely agreed throughout the world.

The African Charter includes a section on the responsibilities of children to their families, communities, and nations.[13] These responsibilities include assisting their families in case of need, and placing their physical and intellectual abilities at the service of their communities, both of which could include economic activity. This is an important addition: people do not have rights without responsibilities, and we see in the stories of many child domestic workers how they respond to the needs of their families.

Neither of these documents speaks directly against the employment of children, but both speak of rights that relate to children's working conditions, including the following key points.

• Where courts, welfare institutions or administrative authorities deal with children, *the child's best interests shall be the primary consideration.*[14]

• Children should *not be separated from their parents against their will* except when competent authorities decide this to be in the child's interests, and then the child should be able to maintain personal relations with both parents.[15]

• Children have the right to access information and *to express their own opinions.*[16]

• Children have the right to *freedom of association* and freedom of peaceful assembly.[17]

• *The child's opinions shall be given careful consideration* in matters that affect their lives.[18]

• All children have a right to the highest attainable standards of *health and health care.*[19]

• All children have *a right to education*, especially primary education, and to further education and training according to their ability.[20]

• *Children shall have time to rest and play* and equal opportunities for culture and artistic activities.[21]

• *States shall protect the child from economic exploitation and work that may interfere with education or be harmful to health and well-being.*[22]

The ILO has been strongly against the employment of children. In 1973, it approved a convention on the minimum age of employment but this was not widely ratified by member states – less than 50 in the first 25 years (although more states have been ratifying it in recent years, when ratification has been linked to certain kinds of aid). In 1999, it approved a convention requiring countries to take immediate steps to stop the 'worst forms of child labour' and this has been quickly adopted by nearly all countries in the world.

All these conventions have been defined by adults. When the African Movement of Working Children and Youth met in Senegal in 1997, and discussed their problems, they affirmed twelve priority rights:

1. the right to read and write;

2. the right to express oneself and get organised;

3. the right to be taught a trade;

4. the right to play and leisure;

5. the right to health care;

6. the right to be listened to;

7. the right to rest when sick;

8. the right to work in safety;

9. the right to be respected and dignity;

10. the right to stay in the village;[23]

11. the right to light and limited work; and

12. the right to equitable justice.

Most of these can be found implicitly in international conventions. But notice that the children are explicit on the kind of education they prioritise: to be taught a trade and to read and write. The children assert their right to appropriate work. In particular, they want chances to earn money in their villages, and not be forced to leave their rural homes to earn money in the cities – expressed as the right to stay in the village. Children should not be separated from the security and care of their families against their will.

The point to note here is that there are international standards that are widely accepted in Africa and throughout the world, regarding the treatment of children.

How we think about children and childhood

It is the responsibility of adults to see that the treatment of children is in accordance with these rights. Not all people, however, think of children as citizens with rights. The way employers treat child domestic workers depends partly on the way they think about children, especially other people's children. In Zimbabwean society there is a variety of stereotypes of children, and attitudes towards children that affect the way adults deal with them. Such stereotypes are not always explicitly acknowledged but are commonly implied in behaviour – including much of the behaviour reported by child domestic workers. Here are some of them:

• Children need guidance and care, not talk about rights.

• Children are ignorant and inexperienced. They should listen to and obey adults. They have no ideas worth hearing.

• Children need to be trained through discipline: it is too late when they are adults. As the proverb says, *'Kurayira kunoda pwere: Mukuru ndimambo.* [24] [Discipline is needed for young children: an adult is a chief.]

• Children (especially child domestic workers) are lazy and careless. The only way to stop them missing their duties or making mistakes is to punish them.

• In these hard times it is every person for himself or herself. Employers assume that children behave accordingly: if children seek employment, they will look after themselves and get away with whatever they can. So employers assume a right to get as much as they can out of the children for as little as possible.

• Child workers come from poor families and do not deserve respect. As the proverb says, *'Mwana wowenzara murasi.* [25] [A child from a place of hunger throws things away.]

• Child workers are of lower status than the children of the household and should remain separate and do different kinds of work.

• Child workers are given better food than they had at home. They should be grateful and work hard and not make further demands on their patrons.

• Other people's children will not look after you in old age, so there is no need to look after them.

All these perceptions of children have some basis in tradition or reality but they are stereotypes. That is, they take a limited aspect of childhood, and assume that it applies to all children at all times. The problem with stereotypes is that they often contain some truth but at the same time, they conceal other aspects of the situation. They draw broad pictures from isolated incidents and do not pay attention to individual characteristics and needs. Because you come across one child domestic who is lazy and irresponsible, this does not mean that they are all like that. In any case, the irresponsible behaviour of the child might be due to the way they have been treated. Children who know that they are being treated badly, especially when their remuneration is insufficient for their needs, may take pride in finding illicit ways to get what they need from their employers.[26] Stereotypes make us feel confident that we understand when in fact we are only touching on the surface. Our behaviour towards children should not be governed by stereotypes, but rather by the value we place on children, and their importance for the future of our society.

In traditional African values children are to be treasured as blessings of God and the ancestors: life without a child is often viewed as meaningless. Children belong not only to their parents but to their kinsmen and community. They provide security in old age and ensure the replacement and growth of the community. They deserve respect as persons. Children are young people, becoming mature, certainly with the help of adults, but ultimately by learning from their experience. We need to ensure that their experience is such that they learn to live in harmony with their social and physical environment, not in pain and fear. They can grow in competence and knowledge if they are guided and encouraged. They can grow in responsibility if they are allowed to make decisions appropriate to their situation. They can grow in maturity if they are encouraged to think. They have experience and knowledge, especially of things that affect their lives, and they deserve to be listened to.

Human society should be different from the world of nature. Among animals, might is right. Unprotected young usually become prey to stronger animals. Animals with disabilities are usually left to die. In human society, we like to think that we are cultured, and so care for each other, and respect each other, in a way that animals do not. We are not supposed to treat people with contempt simply because they need help, whether they are children, or disabled, or simply poor. Unfortunately, culture sometimes fails to curb our aggressive instincts towards those who are weaker than we are. When there are no adults to protect children, some people think that they can do what they like with those children. And child domestic workers consequently suffer, as we shall see in this book.

Children are people. They have feelings that should be respected. They are vulnerable and inexperienced, and need help and support. Children can also think for themselves and show resilience to the problems that face them. We need to listen to them and encourage them as they try and learn to help themselves and to help each other. In programmes that encourage children to do things for themselves, people frequently say that it is amazing how much they can do when they are given space.

Methods

We used a variety of methods to collect information on child domestic workers. General information comes from children contacted through the domestic workers' union. Officers of ZDAWU have been identifying child domestic workers in various towns throughout the country, and have brought them together in small groups to talk about their problems and see what they can do about them. We have met representative children at various workshops for working children and heard the domestic workers' complaints about their work and conditions.

In April of 2003, at a workshop for officers and with contributions from some child workers, we assembled issues that children wanted to raise in a code of practice. We prepared a questionnaire for a survey on their life and work conditions, which we translated into Shona.[27] The questionnaire had both specific questions to be answered, and a number of open questions, to allow the children to say whatever they wished to say about their situation. Tinashe Pfigu and Jeremiah Chinodya visited the various centres in January and February of 2004 to discuss the questionnaire with selected members from each group. These then went back to their groups and helped others to fill in the questionnaire. The return rates were uneven and some of the questions were not well understood or answered in all of the groups. We received 144 completed questionnaires from children, although on particular questions the number of clear answers is often less than this. The children's responses provide an indication of the differences in working conditions and the range of problems they face; as, however, they are based on a non-random sample they do not provide narrowly accurate statistics. In particular, children working under especially harsh conditions can less easily speak to outsiders or join clubs of child domestic workers, for these would be under strict control by their employers who would not allow them to attend group meetings. Consequently, our sample tended to exclude such children although we received some second-hand information about them. Our data are thus likely to be biased towards the more contented children, living in more benign situations.

Tinashe Pfigu was employed by ZDAWU in 2004, to visit all the groups and help them develop their ideas and activities. Among other things, she discussed with the children their views on appropriate work for children of different ages to do in the home, which provided the basis for our recommendations. She has also met with some of the employers and discussed issues with them.

In the second half of the previous year she made more detailed case studies of three child domestic workers. She spent two weeks in each of three homes employing child domestic workers, hearing from both the employers and the employees. In these three cases, we have detailed information on the background and situation of the child workers, and on their relationship with the employers.

In April and May 2004, Rumbidzai Rurevo met with children in Zvishavane, Kadoma, and Harare through the clubs supported by ZDAWU, to collect life stories from a few of them. The plan was to take selected cases from the survey, but it proved difficult to contact these children when she made the visits and it transpired that some of the children in the survey were not regular members of the clubs. She nevertheless collected stories from children who were working in domestic service in these centres. In Zvishavane, she held discussions with groups of children about conditions of work and the way they are treated.

In our presentation, we pay attention to what the children said about their work and their conditions and based on what the children told us, we make many observations. Often we cite their very words (though usually our English translation of what they said). This book is an attempt to accord them the right to have a say on issues that affect their lives and above all, to be listened to.

In all presentations from the case studies, pseudonyms have been used for both the children and their employers, to protect the identities of the children and sometimes of their employers.

The survey sample

Our survey covered 144 children spread over twelve centres.[29] These were all children in urban areas, and we have only one case study of a child in a rural area. The majority (69 percent) was in the age group 15-17 and in this group there were more than twice as many girls as boys. In the younger age groups, the gender ratio is more even..

We asked the children if they were happy in their work. About half (51 percent) responded positively. These replies are likely to represent the current mood of the children rather than their long-term contentment. A child who has recently been scolded and insulted is likely to respond that he or she is unhappy, even if for most of the time they are relatively content. Equally, a child who has recently experienced something pleasant, such as a gift or rise in wages, is likely to express contentment, even if much of the time they are miserable. Nevertheless, the responses indicate that at any one time half the children are content, including most of those below the minimum age for employment (74 percent). A greater number of the older age group are not content with their situations.[30] These older children are likely to be thinking about their futures and see little chance of improving themselves in domestic service. More girls than boys are unhappy.[31] One possibility is that girls, and particularly older girls, are liable to suffer sexual harassment in the household. Although boys sometimes complain of having to do girls' work, the majority are well able to adapt to the situation.

We asked the children to list what they liked about their work and what they disliked. The majority listed items on both sides (and we shall be mentioning some of these later); four did not respond at all to this question. Seventeen (12 percent) listed nothing among the dislikes, with some commenting that they liked everything about their work. Forty-five (31 percent) listed nothing that they liked, again sometimes explicitly commenting that there was nothing good. This is an indication that a significant number of child domestic workers are very unhappy and their livelihoods need to be improved. While we do not advocate abolishing child domestic work, we are concerned that action be taken to improve the situations of many of the child workers.

Our data show the expected statistical correlation between those who are unhappy and those who want to stop working.[32] Nevertheless, a significant number (29) of those who were unhappy in their work wanted their situation to be improved rather than to lose their employment entirely. As one 17-year-old girl explained, although she had no free time, received low pay, slept in the kitchen and was very unhappy, she did not want to leave her job 'because if I stopped working, there is no one who can look after my life'.

Similarly, eighteen of those who are content with their work said they wanted to leave their jobs. Taking into account those who are unhappy in their work and those who want to stop working, we realise that many children are working under some kind of duress, which is a cause for concern.

NOTES

1. See the case studies in Michael Bourdillon (ed.) *Earning a Life: Working Children in Zimbabwe* (Harare, Weaver Press, 2000).

2. See Yotamu Chirwa and Michael Bourdillon, 'Small-Scale Commercial Farming: Working Children in Nyanyadzi Irrigation Scheme', in *Earning a Life*, pp. 127-146.

3. See William E. Myers, 'Can children's work and education be reconciled?' *International Journal of Educational Policy, Research and Practice* (2001), 3, pp. 307-330 (311-312).

4. Save the Children, *Children and Work: Save the Children's position on children and work*. (London, Save the Children, 2003), p. 11.

5. ILO Convention 182, article 3 (a).

6. ILO Convention 182, article 3 (d).

7. See ILO Recommendation 190 of 1999, paragraph 3.

8. See Maggie Black, Child Domestic Servants: Finding a Voice (London, Anti-slavery International, 2002); UNICEF, Child Domestic Works, Innocenti Digest, Issue No. 5 (Florence, UNICEF, 1998). Bharati Pflug argues that the majority of child domestic workers in Asia are working in hazardous conditions: *An Overview of Child Domestic Workers in Asia* (Geneva: ILO, 1995), p.10. Blagbrough & Glynn, 'Child domestic Workers: Characteristics of the modern slave and approaches to ending such exploitation' *Childhood* 6 (1999), 1, pp.51-56. Child domestic workers face severe problems of abuse and disrespect world wide.

9. For example on child domestic workers in West Bengal, see D. Lakshmi Rani and Manabendranath Roy (ed.), *Child Domestic Work: A violation of human rights* (London, Save the Children UK, 2005). The ILO report, *A Global Alliance Against Forced Labour* (Global Report under the Follow-up to the ILO Declaration on Fundamental Principles and Rights at Work: International Labour Conference, 93rd Session, Report I (B), Geneva, 2005, p.9) points out that domestic workers frequently suffer various forms of coercion.Such coercion of child domestic workers identifies their work as one of the worst forms.

10. Maggie Black and Jonathan Blagbrough in UNICEF, *Child Domestic Work*, pp. 14-15.

11.This has not been well documented in Zimbabwe, but see S. Lallemand, *La Circulation des enfants en société traditionnelle. Prêt, don, échange* (Paris, l'Harmattan, 1993); and on South Africa, C.S. van der Waal, 'Rural children and residential instability in the Northern Province of South Africa', Social Dynamics 22 (1996), 1, pp. 31-53.

12. This is a very rough estimate based on the following finding. In Chinhoyi, Wellington Chiparamakura of ZDAWU found 180 child domestic workers taking infants to and from the crèches in the town. We guess that about a third of child domestic workers are involved in this activity, which would mean that there are around 540 child domestic workers in Chinhoyi, or 0.9 percent of the population of the city (59,200). Applying this figure to the urban population of Zimbabwe (3,827,000), we come to a figure of 34,000. We have no way of estimating for the rural areas.

13. Article 31 a & b.

14. CRC article 3.1: AC article 4.1.

15. CRC article 9: AC article 19.

16. CRC article 13, 14: AC article 7.

17. CRC article 15: AC article 8.

18. CRC article 12: AC article 4.2 (see also 7).

19. CRC article 24: AC article 14.

20. CRC article 28: AC article 11.

21. CRC article 31.1: AC article 12.1.

22. CRC article 32.1: AC article 15.

23. This refers to the fact that children are often forced away from home through the absence of facilities or opportunities in the villages, and end up in bad situations away from their kin.

24. M.A. Hamutyineyi and A.B. Plangger, *Tsumo – Shumo: Shona Proverbial Lore and Wisdom* (Gweru, Mambo Press, 1974), no. 997.

25. Id., no. 833.

26. For an example from West Africa, see Mélanie Y. Jacquemin, 'Children's domestic work in Abidjan, Côte d'Ivoire: The *petites bonnes* have the floor', *Childhood* 11 (2004), 3, p. 390.

27. Shona is the native language of the vast majority of the children, although some children in Bulawayo, Gweru, and Zvishavane needed translation into Sindebele, which was done verbally.

28. See Tinashe Pfigu, 'Invisible Workers': a study of child domestic work in Zimbabwe. Dissertation submitted for M.Sc. Degree (Harare, Department of Sociology, University of Zimbabwe, 2004).

29. The composition of our sample can be seen from Table 1 and 2 in the annex.

30. Table 3.

31. Table 4.

32. Table 5.

2

Forms of Engagement in Domestic Work

Help in the home

Most children are expected to provide some help in the home and the amount of work varies with the resources of the family. Well-off families may have hired domestic help and a variety of aids in the home to minimise work, while poorer families cannot afford outside help and have fewer aids. The work of children in such homes may include hours spent fetching and cutting firewood for cooking and fetching water from an external source. In well-off families, the chores assigned to children may be token gestures to cultural values concerning the training of children, whereas in poorer families they are essential to the running of the home.

The household burdens imposed on children are usually particularly harsh on girls. Many tasks such as cooking, cleaning, washing clothes and dishes, fetching water and the care of infants, are considered the responsibility of girls. Boys are unlikely to help in such tasks when girls are present. Consequently, girls in traditional settings often have little time for their own creative activities. The work assigned to boys, such as tending livestock, is usually less onerous and takes up less time than work assigned to girls.[33] These traditional chores are perceived as cultural behaviour rather than work and when working children visit their homes on days off, girls are expected to pick up their usual chores in the household.

Help in the home easily extends to the economic enterprises undertaken by a family. In rural areas children usually help in the fields and young boys are often in charge of livestock. This might extend to leading cattle hired out to plough or draw a cart, for cash. In the urban areas children might be expected to help parents working in the informal sector, in running a stall, for example, or perhaps some kind of craft. Children in urban areas cannot work in the fields but they can contribute to the family's livelihood through other activities that generate cash, even by begging.

In both rural and urban areas, such work sometimes interferes with schoolwork. A girl in a rural home was looking after the household, cooking and caring for her father and younger brothers and sisters while her mother was away sick. The time she spent on family chores amounted to over forty hours a week, making her exhausted and unable to concentrate properly at school. A teenage boy was required to perform chores not only in his own home, but in the homes of his father's brothers. Culturally he could not refuse the requests of these, who are categorised as his fathers. As a result he was working over thirty hours a week during the school term and this affected his schooling.[34] A 13-year-old girl was helping her mother to run a small stall after school hours. While she did not complain, she admitted that she was not always able to complete her schoolwork. She said that her mother needed her help to bring in income for the family and that she was learning a trade that would be useful to her in the future.[35]

In the current economic climate in Zimbabwe, many children have to contribute income for the running of the home. For such children, a cash income supplements the family livelihood as does the work of rural children on their parents' farm. One form of cash income is found in domestic employment, although this does not always achieve the required goals. One of the child domestic workers in our sample complained that his wages were not enough to buy necessities for himself as well as being able to send something home for his mother's other children.

Even in well-off households, children sometimes have so much to do in running the home that their schoolwork suffers. At a private school in Harare, there were several cases of teenage girls being left to run the household while their parents were away for months at the time. Sometimes they had domestic help, but they still had the responsibility of doing the shopping, organising younger brothers and sisters, queuing at the bank, and so on. Teachers learned about the situation when they noticed deterioration in schoolwork. In one case, a girl was sent to live at the home of a sick relative and to care for her, which interfered with the child's school performance. Although these cases did not involve the employment of children for wages, they all involved making demands on children that interfered with their education, more so than some of the cases of child employees.

Another way in which help in the home can disrupt a child's development and social life arises when the child is required to care for the sick. When a parent or other family member is seriously ill, this can be very demanding. While it is admirable for a child to care for a close relative who is seriously ill, such caring work needs support. This is a problem that can arise for any children anywhere[36] but it becomes particularly significant in the context of the HIV/AIDS epidemic.[37]

In principle, there is nothing wrong with children doing this kind of work, but we should be aware of the burden we are placing on them. If their schoolwork suffers, this may jeopardise their future careers. The problem is not that they are required to work to help the family – the problem is how much work they are required to do. Sometimes, there is little choice, such as when parents die and children have to take over the running of the household. Often, however, the burden on children can be reduced, if we take the trouble to notice how much we are requiring them to do.

Helping kin

Apart from working in their own homes, children are sometimes sent to help relatives. This is a second kind of domestic work. When a relative is living on her own and needs help, she may ask her brother or sister to send a daughter to live with her to help. In Zimbabwean culture such a request is legitimate and should not be refused. In an extended family system, children are perceived as the responsibility of the whole family, and as belonging to the whole extended family. Care for children is thus easily shared among kin, as are the services that children can offer. When a child goes to live with kin, he or she is not paid for services, but the senior relative takes responsibility for all the child's needs.[38] This system often provides a wide range of care for children and is a safety net against the inability of parents to care for them. However, it can also result in children being exploited when their needs become secondary to the demands of adults in the family.

Sometimes parents who are poor and struggling send their children to stay with a wealthy relative, where they are treated as part of the family but are expected to earn their keep. Another reason for sending children to relatives may be that the parents are away from home in employment. Sometimes when parents die, the children are spread out among different relatives, where they are looked after but have to earn their keep. Sometimes people are simply following a tradition that children spend time away from home with grandparents or other kin, as part of the traditional system of socialisation and strengthening bonds of kinship.[39]

It is a good thing that members of a family support each other, and provide help when it is needed. It is good for children to grow up learning about their responsibilities to family members. When someone in the family is very sick, it is important to have a relative to care for them. Often the children are willing partners in these arrangements and are happy with them. But sometimes they are forced against their will, and sometimes they find their own lives, and particularly their education, are shattered as a result of the arrangements.

We need to take care that the children also benefit from the arrangements. The following case illustrates this need.[40]

Tariro came to Harare to work when she was 13 years old, and she had been working for two years when we met her. Her father passed away when she was in the fifth grade of primary school. Her father's elder brother took most of what was left by the father, who used to work for Chibuku Breweries. With the little that was left for her mother, they continued living in their rural home, but life was difficult for them as there was no one earning an income. Nevertheless, Tariro completed her seven years of primary schooling and started her first form of secondary school. Her mother was still in the rural areas with Tariro's two younger sisters and one brother. Her two sisters were in primary school and her brother had not started school yet.

Sibongile, a distant relative of her mother, offered to take Tariro to Harare so that she could to go to school whilst helping around the house. The mother readily agreed since her daughter would benefit.

Sibongile was a single mother with twins in grade five of primary school. Tariro had previously met Sibongile on her occasional visits to the rural home.

When they left the rural home for Harare, the second term of the school year was about to start and Tariro was due to continue in form 1. Although there was a secondary school near her Harare home, Sibongile did not look for a place for Tariro. Tariro continued doing her household tasks, but became tired of waiting for a school place. At this time, she was receiving enough money to buy herself sanitary pads and lotion, but no formal wages. When Christmas came, she went to visit her mother. Her mother was not pleased that she was not going to school, although everything else was being provided. She sent Tariro's uncle to talk to Sibongile and some of Tariro's relatives intervened, persuading Sibongile to take Tariro to school. After these talks, Sibongile personally went to Mutare to fetch Tariro. She agreed to send her to school and when schools opened, and Tariro was enrolled into form one.

At the same time, an arrangement was made about payments. Every month-end, Tariro was to be paid $7,000,[41] from which her school fees were paid. Sibongile bought uniforms for the girl to give her a good start. Tariro kept her monthly pay and she learnt how to spend her money to cater for her schooling. Early in 2003, her wages were increased to $10,000 a month. The local school was not expensive and she was able to save from this enough for her school fees every term. Sibongile sometimes bought stationary for her when she was shopping for her twins. Although Tariro was saddened by the fact that she did not have anything to spare to send her mother, she was content as she was going to school and hoped to earn more when she finished school, left Sibongile, and found formal employment.

Tariro's day started very early with some households chores before she dashed to school. Sibongile's children went to school in town so they left with their mother and came back with her after work. Before school, Tariro cleaned the house and made breakfast for everyone. She came back late in the afternoon and quickly did her homework before cooking supper. Sibongile arrived home around 5 p.m., when Tariro had finished her homework and was already preparing dinner. Tariro said that tidying up after dinner was important for her since it made the following day easier. She usually managed about an hour of extra reading after dinner and before retiring to bed. She went to bed early as she said she did not get time to rest during the day because she had many responsibilities around the house. She normally did the laundry twice a week washing the clothes in the evening and hanging them out in the morning or the afternoon if she did not have too much homework. Tariro said she had learnt to work fast and to manage her time, balancing her household chores with her schoolwork. This was how her four busier days of the week were filled.

Morning: 5 - 6.30 a.m.

Cleaning the house and making breakfast: 1 hour

Late afternoon

Homework: 1 hour

Cooking: 2 hours

Laundry or ironing: 2 hours

Evening

Washing Dishes: 30 minutes

Total house-work: 6 hours

On the other three days, there was no laundry and ironing, so reducing her working hours to four, thus giving her load of approximately 36 hours a week. On Sundays, they all went to church. Some Saturdays, Tariro was happy to accompany Sibongile and her children to town, and they went together on most visits to relatives.

Initially, she did not want to work and go to school as well, and feared her schoolwork would suffer. She found, however, that her timetable enabled her to combine housework with schoolwork, and the arrangement provided her with the much-needed opportunity to go to school. She said,

> I am always tired, although I am grateful that I attend school. However, I feel that this is compensated for by the chance I have been given in my life to do something for myself.

She learnt to like her work. She always remembered her mother telling her that this was her gateway to having something better in life.

Sibongile readily helped Tariro if she did not know how to do something or use something. Tariro recounted the time Sibongile showed her how to use her new microwave oven. Sibongile has also tried to assume the role of a mother. Tariro explained that Sibongile expected her to behave well and always emphasised that this was not the time for her to get naughty with boys: that time would come later.

In this case, we see a child from a poor home gaining some advantage by working for someone who was better off. Initially, the arrangement was vague, in the idiom of a relative helping a child and receiving in turn needed help from someone she could trust. As a result, the child received no pay and no schooling. Although the employer was a relative, she needed a visit from Tariro's family to meet her obligations about the girl's schooling, and to come to a formal arrangement concerning wages.

Kin often say that children working for them are family, which means they do not have contracts and do not receive pay for their work. It means they have to work for nothing, at whatever the owners of the house want them to do. Because such helping is not considered to be employment, children are often working at an age very much younger than those who are formally employed.[42] We met one older girl who was sent to help her aunt to run her house, and was given much work, no money, and no time for the night school that she had been promised. She was being treated like a slave. So in the end she ran away to live on the streets.[43] We have also come across children, particularly those living with step-parents, who are physically abused if they do not do all that is required of them, especially if they do not bring home enough money to pay for their keep.

When children go to live with relatives and look after the house to earn their keep, this is another kind of domestic work. These arrangements can work for the benefit of the children and for the family as a whole, but we need to take care that such arrangements do not slip into gross exploitation of disadvantaged children.

Fostering

Apart from sending children to help relatives, another strategy of poor households to maintain their livelihood is the movement of people between households. In particular, children are often fostered with relatives or even friends. In such arrangements, the children receive shelter and food, usually in exchange for services. Sometimes the reason is insecurity in their parental home, or the movement of one or both parents in search of employment. Such coping strategies are important for the families concerned, and may also benefit the children, by providing a home and adult care when their parents are unable to render these.

This strategy fits into a more general pattern of patronage, in which disadvantaged persons receive access to resources in exchange for loyalty and service. People see patronage as a wealthy or powerful person bestowing favours on the poorer person. While patrons can genuinely help clients, they may also use patronage to conceal the exploitation of poor people by making excessive demands on them.

Patronage occurs in a variety of situations. In traditional Shona societies, rulers sometimes gave land to needy individuals or groups of people, in exchange for loyalty.[44] A person needing support from the chief might acquire his patronage by giving him gifts, but while these actions ideally maintain good relations between the chiefs and their peoples, they can easily turn into extortion. A landowner might favour a widow by giving her a place to live and limited land to cultivate. She is likely to speak of his generosity but would not think of refusing her labour when he wanted it, however low the wages may be.[45] Ideally both sides benefit from such relationships, but since the poorer person usually enters the relationship under duress, they have little control over the exchange and exploitation is always possible.[46]

Seeking patronage is a valid strategy for the poor, along with mobility between households. In populations devastated by HIV/AIDS, patronage can be the salvation of many orphans and child domestic work fits readily into this pattern. While the patron receives services from the child, the child receives shelter, nourishment, and sometimes care from the patron.[47] However, child domestic work mingles patronage with exploitation in ways that are not easily disentangled. Where the alternatives for the children are likely to be worse than their domestic employment, it makes sense to take advantage of the patronage, and to persuade the employers to take responsibility for the well-being and development of the children they employ. If we simply focus on the exploitation and the harm that children suffer in domestic employment, there is a danger that impoverished and disadvantaged children will lose one of the few possibilities available for improving their situation.

The following case of a child domestic worker in a rural village illustrates the cultural context in which domestic service can provide foster care and patronage for a deprived child.[48]

Temba was 14 at the time of the research, and living in a village in Chihota District, about 120 km from Harare. His parents died when he was five, and initially his father's brother took care of him, according to custom. Just before Temba started his last year of primary school, his father's brother announced that he had to take care of his own children and could no longer afford to send Temba to school. News spread that Temba had dropped out of school. He pointed out that his father's brother was not cruel, but poor and the few resources he had were not sufficient to send Temba to school.

The village headman was sympathetic towards the boy, who was known to be bright, and he approached the Chanetsa family. Their household comprised only the elderly head of the family, referred to as Sekuru – grandfather, and a younger man, Tendekai, who was employed to take care of the old man, the homestead, and the family's fields. The old man's children were economically well off and they had developed the homestead. The old man had always indicated that he would like some company. The village headman negotiated with one of the old man's sons to take in the young boy and pay his school fees in return for the young boy's taking care of the old man and providing company. This would also ease pressure on Tendekai, leaving him more time for farming, taking care of livestock, and the general management of the household.

By the time he turned 13, Temba had moved into the Chanetsa homestead. Before the old man's son left, he told the boy that he was to be responsible for doing the household chores, but that Tendekai would handle what needed to be done while he was at school.

Temba said he was not complaining about his working conditions because he would have been worse off if he had not been taken in by the Chanetsas. He did not receive what he calls pay, although he received pocket money every month-end when one of Mr Chanetsa's sons visited. He was happy with the arrangement because the school uniforms, the books, and the food he received from the Chanetsas were worth much more than he could have expected to receive in wages. At the time of the study, he was in the first year of secondary school and pointed to his advantage over other children, in that he could read at night by the lighting from the solar-powered system installed in the Chanetsa homestead. Also, Tendekai helped him with the housework and cooking, especially when there was not much work in the fields. He described a typical day's work.

> I usually wake up very early – 5 a.m. – as grandfather wants porridge early in the morning. I prepare his porridge and clean the house. Although the house is relatively big – five bedrooms, I don't have to clean every room every day as there are only the three of us. There is usually not so much dirt lying around also. This makes the task in the morning very easy. The school is a few kilometres away, approximately 3 km. I therefore leave early – about 6:30 a.m. – so that I get to school on time.

> I usually come back in the late afternoon, about 3 p.m. and prepare food for supper. Usually, Tendekai … prepares lunch, or I cook the lunch for Sekuru in the morning if it's in the rainy season, when Tendekai has to do a lot of work in the fields. As I prepare supper, Sekuru usually tells me stories. He has come to rely on me for help in anything and I have come to see him as a guardian. However, at times I miss my peers as I don't live with anyone who is also my age. However, on Sundays, my friends sometimes visit me and we have a great time with grandfather telling us stories and playing football if he is resting. Saturday is usually a time to do the laundry and do any catching up with my work if there is any need. My father's brother provides me with the necessary fatherly advice and visits me three times or more a week, especially after school, as we are neighbours. Being at Chanetsa's homestead has given me the opportunity to keep going to school as I wanted, and to be provided for.

On the days we observed him, his schedule was as follows:

> Cooking porridge, cleaning the kitchen,
> and washing plates: 5-6 a.m., 1 hour
> Help in the fields if there is need: 3-5 p.m., 2 hours
> Preparing dinner: 5.30-6.30, 1 hour
> **Total: 4 hours**

Temba was an employee and in a sense he was also a member of the family. He was an employee in so far as he had a responsibility to take care of the grandfather and do the household chores allocated to him. Nevertheless, he was a member of the family in the sense that he was taken care of by the Chanetsas. The grandfather treated Temba well and said his life had become enjoyable with the boy's company.

Temba remained in the context of his immediate kin, whom he saw regularly. As we shall see, this is an advantage for child workers. His workload was light, and he was able to give full attention to his schoolwork. The arrangement, however, treated Temba as an orphan to be cared for, rather than an employee with rights. Although he had to work, his work was not given an economic value. He had no formal days off, and was expected to be available in the home. He said he missed the company of peers, which a boy of that age could expect to receive.

The fostering relationship can be of great benefit to children. But the difference between fostering and employment can be blurred.[49] In cases like Temba's, the idea of fostering allows people to ignore the fact that this is employment and is subject to the rules that protect the rights of employees.[50] Such employment can become virtually invisible when employers and employees adopt kinship terms to address each other.

Formal employment

Finally, we come to the focus of this book: children who formally contract with an employer to do domestic work. There is great variety in this kind of employment. It can be part-time help, with the child living with his or her family or relatives, and spending a few hours in domestic employment, while still attending school and having time for other social activities. Other children live with strangers far from their homes, with no kin to defend them and support them. Such children are at the call of their employers all day, every day and may have chores that occupy them for more than twelve hours a day. Sometimes the children are not allowed out of the home they are working in (see below) and have no chance to play with children of their own age, still less to attend school.

One problem the children face is that their status of employee is often disguised. In order to get maximum service for minimum cost, employers may try to fuse the employment of child domestic workers with the idea of children helping out. The child is said to be cared for as a member of the family, with no contract to limit the demands made on the work or to specify remuneration.[51]

Sometimes the children are willing partners and actively go out to seek employment. Sometimes they are forced by their families to take up employment for the benefit of the whole family. As we have pointed out, many are happy in their situation and do not want it disturbed, while many others are very unhappy with the way they are treated. Few people have problems with the first part-time scenario. Many of us disapprove of the last scenario, although probably out of courtesy, people often ignore the situation when they see an acquaintance or friend exploiting a child employee in this way – courtesy, that is, to the adult and not to the child.

Most cases lie somewhere between these extremes, as the following case illustrates.[52]

Nomsa was 14 when she started to work. She was living at her rural home with her parents in Zvimba, around 100 km from Harare. When we met her, she had been working for 18 months for Mr and Mrs Madzima in a low-density suburb of Harare. She is the fourth child in a family of six, including four boys and two girls. Both her parents were alive and were peasant farmers. Nomsa said,

> My father has not been able to develop our homestead. He drinks a lot, and there is hardly enough money for all of them [children] to go to school. Only the first born completed ordinary level.

At school, Nomsa only reached the first term of the first year at secondary school, when her father decided that there was no money for her second term. Neither could her older brother in town assist her.

She was still unhappy about dropping out of school when her friend, who was working as a domestic servant in Harare, came to her rural home for Christmas. The friend's employer had told the girl to bring someone from her home to work for the Madzimas. According to Nomsa, when her friend came home during the Christmas holiday, she told Nomsa of the possibility of going to night school if she agreed to go to town to work for the Madzimas. Nomsa saw an opportunity to improve her life and agreed. She was excited to hear about the job offer in Harare's low-density suburb, which seemed an opportunity for a better life and to continue her schooling.

When she was taken to Mrs Madzima's home by her friend, she was impressed by the way she was welcomed and immediately felt at home.

> At first I was afraid, but even though she did not know me at all, she welcomed me like a visitor who had been awaited eagerly.

She was not pleased, however, when she was told that she would live in the cottage away from the main house. The cottage did not provide the comforts she had seen in the main house. What she liked about the cottage was that at 6 p.m., she retired and did not have to go back to the main house for any duties.

The main house had four bedrooms on about half an acre of land. Mr and Mrs Madzima were both in professional employment and lived there with their two children.

Her stay in the cottage was short-lived. After five months, Mrs Madzima's mother came from their rural home because of her poor health. Nomsa was invited to stay in the main house since the grandmother needed round-the-clock attention. A second bed was provided for her in the grandmother's bedroom. This was a positive development in Nomsa's view, since she now shared almost everything with the family. She felt she belonged to the family. She could easily relate to Mrs Madzima's daughter, Thandiwe, who was in her first year of secondary school. This was reflected in the way Nomsa appreciated Thandiwe's stories of school, and in learning games from Thandiwe.

Although an extra burden of work was added by the needs of the grandmother, Nomsa felt that the good food she received was adequate compensation. Also, she did not have to budget for clothes as Mrs Madzima occasionally gave her clothes that previously belonged to Thandiwe. She felt homesick at times, but could not go to her rural home every month end because transport costs were high and she wanted to save some money.

Nomsa made an arrangement with her employer to accumulate her weekly days off (Sundays) for a longer visit to her rural home after three months. She arranged with Mrs Madzima to keep her money until the time she wanted to visit her rural home. She explained, 'I don't really need the money on a daily basis and I don't have people that I visit often.'

The only close relative she was familiar with in Harare was her brother, who visited her occasionally. Mrs Madzima initially scolded Nomsa after her brother visited. She subsequently accepted the visits when Nomsa explained that her brother was the only close relative she had much contact with in Harare. Now Mrs Madzima greets Nomsa's brother and asks about the rest of the family in their rural home. In Nomsa's view, this is a huge change.

Nomsa was given considerable responsibility, taking care of the home for the whole day. She was responsible for making the grocery list and ensuring that the household had all the supplies needed for the family. She asserted her autonomy by having a role to play in the home without the control of Mrs Madzima. This is not the role of a passive and incompetent child.

Although Mrs Madzima occasionally shouted to show her authority when something went wrong, Nomsa learnt to deal with this by keeping quiet at that time and later performing her duties as well as she could. Appreciation shown by Mrs Madzima later gave Nomsa confidence.

Although Nomsa liked her place of work, she was disappointed because it did not offer her a chance to go to school as she had hoped. Mrs Madzima made duvets to sell and Nomsa occasionally assisted with the finishing touches, for which she received a little extra pay. She complained, however, that she did not have enough time to become skilled in sewing.

On a typical working day, Nomsa woke at 5 a.m. She took a bath before cleaning the dining and living rooms. At 6 a.m., she helped the children get ready for school and then prepared breakfast for the whole family. By 7.30, Mr and Mrs Madzima left for work together with the children. Nomsa spent the rest of the day with the grandmother. Her daily duties included washing clothes, cleaning the house, and assisting the grandmother whenever she needed help, for example, in taking a bath. She worked in the garden as required, but not on a daily basis. Observations over a five-day period produced the following daily average of hours of work.

Cleaning the house: 2 hours
Washing: 1 hour 30 minutes
Ironing: 2 hours
Cooking: 1 hour 30 minutes
Working in the field or garden: 3 hours
Helping grandmother to wash and dress: 1 hour
Total: 11 hours

She complained about her heavy workload, which arose partly because her work was never clearly defined. When called to look after the grandmother, she was not relieved of other duties. When the gardener was dismissed, he was not immediately replaced and Nomsa had to take over some of his duties, such as watering the garden and weeding the field in the empty space outside the homestead. Although the field was smaller than the fields in her rural home, and although others were occasionally hired to work the field, Nomsa disliked this kind of work, which was tiring and created a large backlog of housework. This work ceased when a new gardener was hired after about six weeks, reducing her workload to eight hours a day, seven days a week.

Nomsa pointed out that she had a lot of free time to spend talking to the grandmother. She developed a relationship with the old lady, who to some extent filled in for her own absent grandmother. They talked about life, and the grandmother advised Nomsa, encouraging her to behave well, especially in the era of AIDS. Nomsa argued that she took care of everything for the grandmother, who consequently felt indebted and obliged to do something for Nomsa occasionally. When at times Mrs Madzima shouted at Nomsa, the grandmother was quick to stand up for the girl:

If it was not for Nomsa who would take care of the household? Would you manage when you go to work?.

Nomsa admitted that there were certain things she disliked. She comforted herself at times with the thought that work in her rural home during the agricultural rainy season was even heavier. She was grateful for being given a home and being made part of the family. When the time came for her to go to her rural home, Mrs Madzima gave her all her money for the five months she had worked and Mr Madzima assisted her with buying sugar and flour from a wholesale outlet. Still, she would be even more grateful if the Madzimas would make an arrangement for her to do some kind of schooling.

Nomsa was generally happy in her work and her employer was considerate. Nomsa was one of those children who would not like to be stopped from working and to lose her situation – unless something better could be found. Nevertheless, her situation was far from ideal. She was disappointed at having no time or opportunity to study or learn a skill. Her employer initially did not appreciate her need for contact with her brother in Harare. The casual nature of the arrangement between employer and employee meant that the employee received many benefits, but also that her hours of work could be indefinitely expanded. At the time of the study, her hours of work were longer than would be allowed for an adult employee, and she did not receive the days off and leave days required by law for adult employees. Above the hours of work, she was always on call to help the grandmother with small tasks (about which she had no complaints, because she got on well with the old lady). Nomsa had no time for the company of her peers, and her employer sometimes encouraged distance between her daughter and Nomsa.

Employing children is not the same as employing adults. Children often do not have the knowledge and experience to deal with some of the problems they face. They need guidance as they grow towards adulthood. They need education. Employers enjoy the services of children and must take on responsibility for their well-being and growth, especially if the child is living with the employer.

We have to consider what we can reasonably expect of children, and what they should receive in return. The purpose of this book is to point out to employers the things that affect child domestic workers for good and for bad, to help them come to arrangements that work for the benefit of the child as well as themselves.

NOTES

33. See, for example, Pamela Reynolds, *Dance Civet Cat: Child Labour in the Zambezi Valley* (Harare, Baobab Books, 1991), pp. 87-89.

34. See Jackie Mungoma and Michael Bourdillon, 'The work of children in impoverished families', in *Women, Men and Work: Rural Livelihoods in South-eastern Zimbabwe* (ed.) Paul Hebinck and Michael Bourdillon (Harare, Weaver Press, 2003), pp. 13-36.

35. Virginia Mapedzahama and Michael Bourdillon, 'Street workers in a Harare suburb', in *Earning a Life: Working Children in Zimbabwe* (ed.) Michael Bourdillon (Harare, Weaver Press, 2000), pp. 31-33.

36. See, for example, Chris Dearden and Saul Becker, *Young Carers in the UK* (London, Carers National Association, 1998).

37. See Elsbeth Robson., 'Invisible carers: Young people in Zimbabwe's home-based health care', in *Earning a Life*, pp. 109-126.

38. In some societies in West Africa, the guardian is also obliged to provide substantial gifts, even dowry, at the end of the service. See Jacquemin, 'Children's domestic work in Abidjan...', p. 384.

39. In some societies, over a third of children are even today brought up away from their parental home. See Erdmute Alber, 'Grandparents as foster-parents: transformations in foster relations between grandparents and grandchildren in northern Benin', *Africa* 74 (1), 2004, 28-45.

40. Adapted from Tinashe Pfigu, 'Invisible Workers' pp. 16-20.

41. In the context of high inflation in Zimbabwe, it is hard to give a value to the national currency. At that time, the official exchange rate was around Z$55 to US$1. The black market rate was around Z$1000 to US$1. A realistic purchasing value was somewhere between, nearer to the official rate for basic commodities produced locally, and close to the black market rate for imported goods. The value of the Z$ had deteriorated considerably by the time of our survey a year later, which we discuss below.

42. In a study in Zambia, 14 out of 76 children working for relatives were below the age of twelve. See Omolara Dakore Oyaide, *Child Domestic Labour in Lusaka: A Gender Perspective – The Case of Kamwala, Kabwata, Libala, Chilenje, Woodlands Extension, Nyumba-Yang* (available at http://www.unicef.org/evaldatabase/files/ZAM_00-004.pdf).

43. Rumbidzai Rurevo and Michael Bourdillon, *Girls on the Street* (Harare, Weaver Press, 2003), pp. 29-31.

44. See M.F.C. Bourdillon, *Shona People* (Gweru, Mambo Press, 1987), p. 105.

45. I provided examples of this in 'Child labour and tea in Zimbabwe'. Paper presented to a conference on Children in the Places, Brunel University, U.K.,

21-23 June, 2001.

46. We should notice that relations between donor agencies and the people they help can often be categorised as patronage.

47. Thérèse Blanchet points out that employers of child domestic workers in Bangladesh see themselves as saviours of poor children, and that there are parallels between employment and adoption or fostering. *Lost Innocence, Stolen Childhood* (Dhaka, The University Press Limited, 1996), pp. 102-103.

48. Adapted from Pfigu, *'Invisible* Workers', pp. 20-23.

49 See Tone Sommerfelt (ed.) *Domestic Child Labour in Morocco* (Oslo, Fafo, 2001), p. 25.

50 See White's and Indrasari's comment that in Indonesia people use the argument of kinship to exempt child domestic service from the normal rules of employment, even though the majority of children are not related to their employers. Ben White and Indrasari Tjandraningsih, *Child Workers in Indonesia* (Bandung, Akatiga, 1998), pp. 28-29.

51. For a similar situation in West Africa, see Jacquemin, 'Children's domestic work in Abidjan…', p. 385.

52. Adapted from Tinashe Pfigu, *'Invisible* Workers', pp. 10-16.

3

Reasons for Seeking Employment

Relatively wealthy children sometimes seek part-time jobs for extra spending money and independence, or for a new experience, sometimes to be shared with their peers. In many situations working children find enjoyment and company in their work.[53] Domestic work, however, offers little in the way of new experiences and is usually lonely for the worker. Occasionally, a child from the rural areas may choose domestic work in the cities for its access to a more exciting life, but usually children are driven into this kind of employment for other reasons.

Choice and Duress

In the survey we asked the children, 'Did you want to work or were you forced to do so?' Nearly three quarters (71 percent) of our sample of 144 child domestic workers said they wanted to work. They spontaneously sought employment. Most of the remainder were pressed into employment by a parent or relative. A number of these were living with relatives and appeared to be orphans and in these cases, the pressure came from the guardian. The deaths of supporting adults, particularly in the current HIV/AIDS epidemic, compel many children to enter employment even when not pressed by a guardian.

I first consider children who are working because they chose to do so, and are quite happy in their work – although they may comment on low pay and long hours. In some cases, the work gives the children a sense of achievement and pride.

A 12-year-old girl in Zvishavane works as a live-in domestic for around four hours a day, washing dishes, sweeping, scrubbing, and polishing the house. She had this to say:

> Where I work, I am happy because I am bringing in money.
> I also have enthusiasm for my work. I have days for resting,
> when I visit relatives and friends. My wish is that you elders
> help us to ensure that we continue to be treated well where

we work.

Another commented:

> I am happy where I work because I bring in money. I have enthusiasm for my work and energy and ability. I am given all that I want by my employers. I eat what I need every day.

Some older children took for granted that they should be in employment. When asked if they wanted to stop work, several responded, 'What would I do?' A 16-year-old girl is happy in her work, although she works around 10-11 hours a day. She commented,

> What will I do if I stop working?

A 14-year-old boy, living with his father and working around five hours a day, explained why he did not want to leave his job:

> There is no other place where I could find work.

A 17-year-old girl commented that she did not want to be like an unemployed person. Another girl who was unhappy with her situation, wanted to leave and find better employment.

Even younger children sometimes like to work for a wage. A 13-year-old girl lives with her father in Zvishavane and works for a relative of her mother (*mainini*). She continues to go to school, but complains of being beaten and scolded at work. Nevertheless, she is happy to work because she gets enough to eat, is paid each month, and can buy what she needs.

We pointed to children's right to have a say in decisions that affect their lives. This implies that children's opinions about whether or not they want employment should be taken seriously. This does not mean, however, that if children choose to work (or not to work), we should simply accept their decision. We do not accept their wishes if children refuse to work at school, or if they choose to engage in drugs or prostitution. We know that such a refusal, or engagement in these activities, can destroy their lives. Similarly, we need to ensure that when children are in employment, their lives are not jeopardised.

When we asked children to give reasons why they do not want to stop working, we realise that some choose to work under duress. The Shona verb, *kuda*, covers a range of desires from serious need, through wants and preferences, to mild likes or wishes. When children say they do not want to leave their work, it might be that they are happy, but in some cases it is because employment fulfils important needs and they see no alternative. Thus one 17-year-old girl, who comes from a small-scale farming family, said she likes her work and she appears to be happy in her situation. Nevertheless, she said she wants to stop work, explaining that she would like to go back to school if she had the means.

A 13-year-old boy in Zvishavane explained his predicament.

> I wish I could buy some clothes. For my part I am troubled to find the money that I am working for. I am troubled to get the things that other children get. I would like to have money and become a person who finds things that will help in the future. I want to find work in the open that I can do on my own like some men, not a person who works in the house. If God helps me, I will pass at school and have a respectable life, not being given work that I do in the house with a grievance.

On the other hand, several children who were clearly unhappy with their work and living conditions said that they did not want to stop working. A 16-year-old girl from the rural district of Buhera was working in the Dzivaresekwa suburb of Harare, for only $3,000 a month and found nothing she liked in her work. She did not like going to bed while she was still hungry, getting up while it was still dark, having to sleep with only one blanket in winter, having no jersey to wear, not being treated like the others. But she did not want to leave her job,

> because if I stopped work, I would have nowhere to go.

She explained,

> My parents do not have enough money to send me to school. They do not find enough food... I have younger brothers and sisters at school. I want to help them as well but the money is not enough to do this.

A 17-year-old girl, who has no father, does not like her work because both her employers, husband and wife, make her work hard and scold her often. But she cannot leave her job.

Several of the children mentioned specific benefits from their work as reasons for staying on in their employment.

> I need the money to eat.

> This is where I can find money to buy clothes.

Several children pointed out that that their work provided for their schooling, even while it might interfere with their performance (a topic we shall discuss later). One 18-year-old boy showed his sense of responsibility to his family. Although he complained of being scolded frequently and being treated like a slave, he said that some things are good. He does not want to leave work

> because this is where the money comes from for my younger brother to go to school.

A boy in Zvishavane could not go to secondary school for want of money. While he is generally happy in his work, he would like something better.

> My wish is that I could find a job that would allow me to help my parents in their farming. But if God helps me, I will find a big job which means I will be able to take care of myself.

If we look in the case studies at the situations that lay behind the children seeking employment, we can better understand the forces behind their choice. There are three common themes that are not mutually exclusive; poverty, broken families, and death or sickness in the family.

Poverty

The children themselves often point out that the reason behind their working is poverty.

Jackie was 16 and working in a relatively wealthy Harare suburb. Her employer treated her with suspicion and kept all food in the house carefully locked away. She worked long hours, but did not complain to anyone about the way she was treated. She blamed this on her background and resigned herself to her fate.

> Those who are poor will always be poor: there is nothing I can do to change that. Even if I decide to leave and look for another job I might encounter the same problem, so I won't have solved anything.

Where facilities at home are few, the attractions of an income from employment are greater. The cases of Nomsa, Temba, and Tariro illustrate this point and there were other similar cases.

Monica was 16 and came from a family of four in Mount Darwin, where her parents still lived as small-scale farmers. She was the youngest, her two elder sisters were married and the brother was at home, helping parents with their farming. Monica stopped going to school when she was in form 2 because the family could not afford to pay her school fees.

Monica found employment through a cousin working in Harare. His friends were looking for a maid and he recommended his cousin. The employers gave him the money for the bus fare, which he sent to her.

Similarly, in the urban areas, employment of children can help overcome difficulties in raising school expenses.

Tawanda was 16, the second child in a family of six. He started working three years earlier, in his last year of primary school, when both parents were out of employment and the family could no longer pay his school fees.

Tawanda's father found him this job. He talked to fellow church members, telling them that he was unemployed and was having problems paying school fees for his children, and meeting the needs of the family. He wanted someone who could employ Tawanda and his sister on a part time basis so that their education would not be interrupted. Tawanda explained that both children wanted to work in order to earn money for school fees and meet other school requirements. Mr and Mrs Mashoko were willing to take Tawanda on as a part time gardener while he continued with his education. Tawanda's aunt (mother's sister) took on his sister, who was also working while still at school. When she went to her aunt's, she was told that she would just be helping around the house – she was not formally employed.

His father subsequently found employment, and so Tawanda could consider leaving his job. Prior to this, Tawanda had difficulties with his employer, but when these were sorted out with help from the union officer, he decided to go on working. He could work and go to school, so it would better to continue with the income so that the family could buy things they could not otherwise afford.

In this case, the child's employment was initiated by necessity, when his father was unemployed. In an ideal situation, it would have been better to find employment for the father. But even when the father did find employment and the necessity was no longer there, the child chose to continue his work because of the perceived benefits of employment.

We might also notice in the last case the difference between the situations of the brother and the sister. Both started working for another household to resolve the difficulty of school expenses. But the girl's work was with kin, and defined as 'helping out', without a formal contract or formal payment.

Peter was born, the youngest of four children, 17 years ago in the lowveld sugar-growing area in the south of the country. His parents divorced when he was young and they are both alive. His father remarried and continued to work in the estates, while his mother sold fruits and vegetables at the market of the small town of Zvishavane. Two of his siblings lived in Harare and the other in Bulawayo, while he stayed with his mother in two rented rooms. Peter is in his fourth year of secondary school.

Peter decided to work to help his mother meet the school expenses. While she was able to pay school fees, it was very difficult to meet other needs like books and uniforms, together with food and clothes. Peter's uncle had a friend who was looking for a gardener and Peter was willing to work in order to supplement his mother's income. Even though his brothers were working, they had their own family commitments and so could not provide regular support. His father provided no support.

Peter ate with his employers, and sometimes slept at their house if he was working late. He said his employers used to treat him badly, making him work long hours and shouting at him for nothing. They did not allow him visitors for fear that they would steal. But things improved after a visit by the officer from the Zimbabwe Domestic Workers' Union.

Peter commented that working was the only option for the poor. Working had enabled him to continue with his education and also to afford some luxuries. He was happy that his employer showed appreciation whenever he had done something good. He commented,

These days you cannot say I failed to go to school because there was no one to pay my school fees. You should also take the initiative and then people will also be willing to help you, in the same manner that God helps those who help themselves and so do people. My work schedule does not interfere with my education because as children we are by law required to work only 6 hours a day, so I have made an arrangement with my employer that I do my work after school. I can read after school and work, when I am off duty and weekends.

Sickness and death in the family

Frequently, poverty is exacerbated by the break up of the family. Of those who were forced to work, compared with those who voluntarily sought to work, a lower proportion (29 percent against 40 percent) had been living with both parents before they started work. This suggests[54] that the chances of being pressurised into working are greater in families where parents have broken up, or where one or both have died.

Since we did not have an adequate support mechanism for the children, we did not ask sensitive questions about whether their parents were alive or dead. Nevertheless, in eight of the eighteen case-studies, children volunteered the information that they sought employment after the death of one or both parents. In a further case, the boy's father was very ill and could do nothing, while his mother spent much time nursing the sick man, putting pressure on the boy to accept the offer of a job. In the survey, we asked the children with whom they had been living before they started work. Only a third had been living with both parents.[55] Although not all of these involved death in the family, many did and this suggests a link between child employment and the AIDS epidemic.

The case of Tariro illustrates what can happen to a child on the death of her father, especially when relatives claim inheritance of his property. We notice that her troubles started when her father died. There are many such examples.

Sophie was a 16-year-old girl, who for over four years had been a domestic worker while still going to school. She had three young siblings who were living in their rural home around 200 kilometres away, with her paternal grandparents. Her father had five other children by different women, so it was very unlikely that she could receive help from her father's relatives. She was grateful that they had agreed to look after the younger ones while she and her mother tried to earn a living.

> When I was in grade 5 my father passed away and I had problems with paying school fees. My mother could not manage to look after the family. Since we were four and I being the first child in the family, so I decide to look for a job.

She did not go to school for a term because her mother was only selling vegetables to earn a living, and could not raise enough money to send her children to school. Being the eldest of the 4 children, Sophie at first helped her mother on her vegetable stall, but they were failing to make ends meet. Also with the mother not so well, Sophie decided to look for a job as a domestic worker.

Godwin was born in Gokwe 16 years ago, the second in a family of four children. His father was a general factory worker in the small town of Kadoma, but died in January 2003, when Godwin was supposed to begin his secondary schooling. The pension was very little, and his father's sister took some of the money left by Godwin's father. They had land at their rural home but no draught power, so that if they returned there, they would not be able to cultivate their land on their own and would have to work for others, in exchange for ploughing.

The three younger children were all out of school, and are living with their mother who made a living by selling firewood – a trade that did not bring in enough to pay school fees. His elder brother was working as a gardener and was the one who found Godwin a job. Godwin was not sure whether his mother had ever tried to obtain help from the Department of Social Welfare.

Godwin worked as a gardener for his employers, and sometimes cooked for them. They provided accommodation. He claimed that they did not pay him cash, but sometimes gave him old clothes. They provided food:

> We don't eat the same meals, I use the same mealie [maize] meal as them but relish is never the same. I am usually given vegetables whilst they eat meat. They say if I want to eat meat, I should buy it for myself.

They did not allow him time off, but he was reluctant to make a formal complaint against his employers, explaining,

> My brother has been with his employers for a very long time and he always says that I should work hard. I was scared of complaining in case they thought I was lazy or lying. I did not want to be a failure; I wanted to emulate my brother. If I do anything wrong they shout at me and I am not given food that day as a way of punishing me.

One point touched on by this case is the traditional inheritance system operating among most ethnic groups in Zimbabwe. Relatives of a dead man claim rights to his property, superseding the rights of the wife. In a village setting in the past, the family of the dead man would have been expected to take on the responsibility of caring for the widow and children of their kinsman. In modern urban settings, however, kin usually live away from the bereaved family and neglect this responsibility. We have come across cases when bereaved orphans are left destitute when greedy kin of their late father take everything that the family possessed.

Another point to notice is how the child was afraid to complain about his situation. He was trying to follow the role model set by an older member of his family and did not have the confidence or experience to see that his situation gave him grounds for complaint. The employer had no objections to the child being interviewed and confidently expressed her view that the child was happy and had no complaints.

The next case is another illustration of difficulties encountered after the death of the man of the house.

Danny was 14 years old and worked as a part time gardener while he was going to school. He was the youngest of seven children in the family. He alone lived with his mother. His father died when he was in grade six and his mother said she could not afford to send him to school, as she was not formally employed. She talked to her relatives about her problem and one of her brothers offered to take him on as a gardener while he continued to attend school. His uncle and aunt were both formally employed.

Things can be even harder when both parents die.

Brilliant was 17 and one of two children. His father died when he was very young, he does not remember him. When his mother became ill, they moved in with her parents and she eventually died when Brilliant was 13. His grandfather worked as a general hand in a local garage and food outlet and was taking care of two children of his own, as well as six other grandchildren whose parents had died, or had divorced and remarried to spouses who did not wish to care for step-children. The eleven people shared a two-roomed house.

After the death of Brilliant's mother, his grandfather suggested that Brilliant look for a job in order to raise money for school fees. The grandfather talked to a workmate who was willing to take Brilliant on as a part-time gardener while he continued his studies. When we met him, he was in the third year of secondary school, and his school fees were paid from the money he received from working as a gardener.

This case illustrates the growing pressure on elderly grandparents, when a number of their children die leaving orphaned grandchildren. In Brilliant's case, the grandfather had a regular income. Others were even less fortunate.

Mandla started working at the age of 14, shortly after both his parents died in 1998, when he was doing grade seven. He continued schooling for a year after the death of his parents and dropped out during the first term of his first year in secondary school. His paternal grandfather, who was an informal wood-worker, was looking after him. He said of his grandfather and elder siblings,

> they wanted me to go to school but they had no means.

Mandla dropped out of school not only on account of school expenses, but also because there was not enough to eat at home. After staying at home for almost a year, his grandfather suggested that Mandla look for a job so that he could find means of looking after himself and helping his grandfather with the welfare of the family. The grandfather found him his first job.

The problems often arise before a parent dies. Brian came from a large, poor family. Although both parents were still alive, he had moved into employment when his father became ill.

Brian was 16 years old, the ninth child in a family of ten. His father used to repair bicycles before he became sick and bed-ridden. Brian's parents were of Mozambican origin and they did not have close relatives in Zimbabwe. Brian used to help his father with the repair work, and when his father became ill, Brian was able to continue the work on his own. Brian's mother was a housewife and was nursing her husband, since he was unable to do anything for himself. Except for his sister, who sold firewood for a living, Brian's siblings were not working or doing anything besides drinking and entertaining in the beer halls (they danced to entertain people: they would be given money for their dancing, which they then drank away).

There was no one who could finance Brian's education. Although he was mending bicycles after school, he was not making enough money to fund his education and that of his young brother, as well as to supplement the family's food. One day a customer, Mr Dzingwa, approached him with a bicycle that needed to be mended and upon collection, he started talking to Brian, enquiring about his welfare, and where he had learnt the trade. After establishing Brian's circumstances Mr Dzingwa asked if Brian would be interested in working for him doing garden work and household chores, while he continued with schooling. Brian said he was interested but he had to consult his parents first. He then started working for the Dzingwas in October 2003. At first, he was responsible for gardening, cleaning the house, scrubbing the floors, washing the dishes, and sometimes even cooking. When he started, he was attending school regularly.

Subsequently, he was moved to manning a tuck-shop owned by Mr Dzingwa, where the hours were long and interfered with his schoolwork. He was not allowed to bring his schoolwork to the shop and was treated with suspicion by the owner. He was not paid for his work, and eventually left. When we met him, the union was trying to help him obtain the money he was owed.

Broken homes

The case of Peter (above) illustrates how poverty can be exacerbated by the break-up of the family. Death is particularly traumatic when a child is living with a single parent who dies.

When we met her, Kundai was 18 years old and working as a housemaid. Her parents were not married and had long been separated. Kundai's mother was despised by both families. She died in 2000 and Kundai's father died in January 2004. After her mother's death, Kundai lived with her maternal grandmother, who was too old to work and was constantly sick.

Her uncles tried to drive her from her grandmother's house, saying that she should go to her father. She went there but her father and his wife did not welcome her. She said that they gave her much work to do, blamed her if anything went wrong, and frequently beat her. Eventually she ran away and went back to her grandmother, explaining,

> We might not have had money or enough food to eat at my grandmother's house, but at least we were happy.

She dropped out of the first year of secondary school.

> My grandmother did not have enough money to send me to school and since my parents had separated, my father's relatives were not willing to look after me.

Kundai's grandmother found her a job so that she could take care of her own needs, and would also in turn help her grandmother. In this job, her tasks included looking after the baby, cleaning the house, some gardening, and attending to all the needs of her employer's sister, who was terminally ill. These needs included bathing her, feeding her, and cleaning up when she soiled her bedding through diarrhoea or vomiting. Kundai developed a fond relationship with the sick lady, who received little help or sympathy from her kin. (The employer argued that the poor were frequently in contact with the sick and dying, and so these nursing tasks were nothing special for Kundai.) Apart from Kundai's heavy workload, her wages were often late in coming and sometimes not paid in full. So she left her job.

Even though the experience had been an unfair and traumatising, Kundai could not afford the comfort of staying at home to recover from the experience. There was not enough food and so her grandmother talked to people she knew and found her grandchild another job, which also involved much work and problems with wages.

We notice that in spite of her problems with her employers, she still chose this in preference to the work that was imposed on her by her father and step-mother.

Even without death in the family, the break up of homes can put pressure on children to fend for themselves. There is often tension between children and step-parents, when the spouse of a parent feels no responsibility for, and often resentment towards, the spouse's children by another man or woman. The next case shows a step-mother who was kind and another who was not.

Alice completed her O-levels, but did not do well and wanted to re-sit them. Her parents separated when she was five years old. With her younger sister, she was left in the custody of her father for a short time, but he used to drink a lot and did not take good care of the children. The mother took them away, but when the father remarried they had to go and live with their father again. Alice said her step-mother was very nice to them but she died after a year. She went back to live with her mother, but after two years the father remarried and took her once more. She did not like her new step-mother, who used to treat her badly. She ran away and went back to her mother, where she stayed for over two years and completed her secondary schooling to O-level. Then her mother died and she went to live with her mother's young sister in another town.

Alice was the eldest of the four children from her father's several marriages. Only the youngest was the child of the current step-mother, and she was worried about the other two. They were still at school, and the fees were being paid from a fund for orphans. She decided to look for a job because her father was no longer taking care of her and because she wanted to raise enough money to re-sit her O-levels, as well as meet other school requirements of her sisters.

Sharon was born 17 years ago. Her parents were never married and she grew up with her maternal grandmother. Both parents subsequently married other partners. While Sharon was in touch with her mother and her husband, she was not in close contact with her father because when she visited him once, she was not received well by her step-mother. Sharon was not able to continue with her education after completing the second year of secondary school. Her step-father was not interested in paying her school fees and since her mother is a housewife in their rural home, she could not raise enough money for her daughter's education. Sharon once tried to live with them, but her step-father was not happy and her presence created tension in the marriage. Sharon was sent to live with her grand-mother in order to save her mother's marriage.

While she was living with her grandmother, the latter's sister came to visit and said she could find Sharon a job, which would keep her out of mischief and bring in money to look after herself. The grand-mother's sister was a domestic worker in Harare and found Sharon a similar job there.

Again and again, we find children being forced out of school and into employment when the family breaks up. In all these stories, employment is not the cause of leaving school. Rather it is perceived as the best option available, and in some cases, provides the possibility of continuing with school.

NOTES

53. When child workers in Paraguay were asked what they liked most about their lives, the most popular response was their jobs, well ahead of school. See Duncan Green, 'Child workers of the America', *Nacla Report on the Americas* 32 (1999), 4, p. 29.

54. Suggests rather than proves: a c2 test gives a probability of 0.25, which is not conclusive.

55. Table 6.

4

Finding a Job

Having decided that employment offered an opportunity to improve their very difficult situations, many children (26 percent in the survey) found employment through their own initiative, which was easier for those who already lived in the area in which they were working. We have met the examples of Brian, who arranged to work for a customer of his father's, and Sophie, who at the age of twelve decided to find employment to help her mother.

Sophie announced at church that she was looking for a job as a house-girl and if anyone knew of someone looking for one they should let her know. An elder in church told her that her neighbour was looking for a house-girl and introduced her to the neighbour. With the consent of Sophie's mother, they agreed that she could start work immediately and also continue with her schooling.

The majority of children in our survey were helped to find employment by parents (24 percent), relatives (38 percent), or friends (8 percent), as we have seen in most of the cases that we have introduced.[56] Often it is the guardian of the child who finds employment. Where the child is in a rural area, it is often a relative already working in an urban area who has the contacts to find the child a position.

Seven children from the survey procured their jobs through an 'agent', that is someone not known personally to them. Agents included relatives of friends, someone in their church, a landlord, the ZDAWU officer, and in one case, a travelling lady who visited a girl's home in rural Hwedza and brought her to work in the Harare township of Chitungwiza.

This last case was a 15-year-old girl, who had been living with her poor rural parents. She did not want to work, but was forced to take the job by her mother. Her younger sister was also working. She had finished primary school, and was no longer going to school. She was unhappy where she worked, did not like the way she was treated with contempt, and would like to find another job that was going to help her in life. Her father visited her once to see that she was alright, but she sees no one else whom she knows (we shall return to the importance of contact with kin). Although this is the only case in our sample of internal trafficking of child workers, such practices are commonly spoken of. While employment can sometimes benefit children from poor families in poor regions, the people involved need to take care that the child is properly cared for, and maintains contact with his or her family.

There is international agreement that all efforts must be made to stop trafficking of children from one country to another to be used as a pliant labour force, or worse. Nevertheless, people do not so readily pay attention to the movement of children within a country to provide pliant labour, which is also a form of trafficking and serious when the child cannot maintain contact with his or her family. The African Movement of Working Children lists as one of the key rights of children their right to stay in the village. This refers to children of poor families being forced to leave their homes in search of an income in the cities. They want projects that provide income in their home villages, to enable children to remain with their families and communities. When children move from rural areas to work in the urban areas, they are likely to feel insecure, lacking knowledge of city life, and far from support that could enable them to assert their wishes or their rights in any way.

While the trafficking of children for labour in Zimbabwe is relatively rare at present, people need to be aware of the harm that children can suffer in such a practice. In West Africa, the trafficking of children has grown to be a matter of major concern.[57] If it is tolerated on a small scale, in a situation where the economy is shrinking and reign is given to private initiatives, it could quickly grow to affect large numbers of children.

Reasons for employing children

Essential to finding employment is someone willing to employ a child. In many of the cases we have seen, the child found work with a relative or an acquaintance, who was willing to help the child out in exchange for part-time service. Concern for children who need help is often genuine and the service may help the child's self-esteem by raising the child above the status of being a beggar. A formal or informal contract also gives the child some security by putting an obligation on the employer. The relationship between the child and the helping adult is more secure when there is a genuine exchange between them.

Apart from the fact that some poor children need help, there are advantages to employers in employing children. Children are usually more pliant than adults, and often more trustworthy (partly because they are more dependent). This has already been illustrated in the case of Godwin, who was afraid to complain about the way he was treated.

Children from rural areas are likely to be particularly pliant when working in the urban areas since they cannot easily leave their job if they are dissatisfied. They can be paid less, often on the grounds that they know little about urban cooking and housekeeping and have to be taught everything. They are often timid and uncertain of themselves. For these reasons employers sometime prefer rural children, avoiding the more assertive behaviour of urban children.

The employer of Nomsa was explicit in that she was following the advice of a workmate that young girls make better maids than do adults supplied by employment agencies. The latter could not be trusted as there are many stories, some of which even appear in the newspapers, about them stealing and brutally treating very young children. A young maid can be taught the day-to-day running of the household over some time, as she has taught Nomsa.

> She can run the household in my absence. Also, she is obedi-
> ent to me, as if I'm her mother or elder sister.

She pointed out that older domestic workers might feel that they are the same age or older than the employer and so cannot easily accept orders.

In the ideal employment situation, the child is provided with income and support in exchange for light work that does not interfere with the child's development and especially with their education. As in all human relationships, there should be exchange in which both parties benefit.

The idiom of helping out children in need, however, can conceal a situation where the exchange is very one-sided and the child is grossly exploited. Kundai's employer (mentioned above) justified her failure to pay the girl's wages in full:

I used to give her food, somewhere to sleep using my blankets, bathing with my soap. She used to eat food that she had never tasted before in her life. Where do the poor get the money to buy eggs or sausages? On top of that you want me to pay her lots of money, as if I was not doing enough for her.

The girl's work included looking after the house and garden, minding the baby, and nursing a dying woman.

Children should be protected from such exploitation, while potential employers who are genuinely concerned to help children in need, should be encouraged.

NOTES

56. Table 8.

57. See UNICEF, *Child Domestic Work*, p. 5.

5

Employing Child Domestic Workers

In what follows, we pay attention to what the children say about their work, particularly in response to our questionnaire survey, which covers a broad range of child domestic workers.

Age of the worker

The minimum age for employment in Zimbabwe is 15 years.[58]. Many (28 percent) of the children in our sample were below this age. We have pointed out that the majority of these younger children are content in their jobs and wish to work. Our cases provide examples of children who appear to have benefited from employment below the legal minimum age.

In discussions, the children themselves argue that no children under the age of twelve should be employed – this used to be the minimum age of employment before it was amended in 1999.[59] Some of them spoke from the experience of having been employed below this age. They felt that very young children should not be expected to take on responsibilities outside their own home. They argued, however, that above the age of twelve children can benefit from employment in tasks appropriate to their age (we discuss these below).

Willingness to work

We noticed that although the majority of the child workers wanted to work, some were pressurised to work by their guardians. Most of those who did not want to work were not happy in their jobs, although this did not apply to all.[60] At one workshop, the children pointed out that children are sometimes forced to work and the work they are made to do hurts them: they do not derive satisfaction from forced work.

'Forced or compulsory labour' is a practice similar to slavery[61] and is classified internationally as among the worst forms of child labour. The line may be difficult to draw between practices similar to slavery on the one hand, and legitimate compulsion on children to do limited work (such as school work or necessary household chores) on the other. Nevertheless, where substantial work is involved, it is incumbent on employers as well as guardians to see that both the children and the guardians are willing partners, and agree to the arrangements being made.

Internationally, domestic work often involves coercion. Sometimes a child is forced to work to repay a family debt. Sometimes the worker is attracted to employment with promises of a better life, and then prevented from returning home when dissatisfied with the conditions. Sometimes a child is forced to work to satisfy kinship obligations. Even when the child is a willing partner to the initial agreement, coercion can take over at a later stage. The child can be prevented from leaving when the employer withholds money due to the child. Extra work and overtime can be imposed on the child, who is often afraid to object.

Contact with family and relatives

Children have the right to maintain relations with both their parents. One of the reasons why the African Movement of Working Children asserted their right to remain in the village is the importance of regular contact with close family and kin. It is often stressful for a child to live far from the people he or she knows. Such effective isolation can be psychologically harmful, bringing the work situation into the category of the worst forms of child labour.

A few of the children (12 percent of the survey sample) were working for employers to whom they were related, although, as we saw in the case of Tariro, this on its own does not guarantee good treatment. More children (31 percent) were working for people who were known to their families. The chances of children being happy in their work were significantly greater if they were working for someone previously known to their family.[62] There were exceptions. A 16-year-old girl wanted to work and her grandmother found her a placement with some people she knew. The girl complained that she was scolded and beaten, given one meal a day and treated like a prisoner (*musungwa*).

The majority (58 percent) were working for people who were not known to their families and were less likely to be happy in their work.[63] For these, contact with kin is particularly important.

In our sample, some children were already living in the areas where they found employment. Others came from far away, usually from rural areas.[64] Those who were working within walking distance of their previous home were slightly more likely to be happy in their work, but distance was not otherwise significant. Notwithstanding what we said about internal trafficking, in our sample, distance from home appeared to make little difference to whether or not the children were happy in their work.

What was significant was whether or not the children were regularly visited by relatives at their place of work.[65] We saw the importance of a visit by relatives to ensure that Tariro was sent to school and paid properly, as well as the importance to Nomsa of visits from her brother. Children have a right to maintain their relations with their parents and family. In one survey case, a child complained that she was not able to visit her mother when she received news that her mother was sick. It is important that a child's family takes the trouble to visit and make sure that the child is faring well in the place of work.

Some employers, however, discourage their child employees from having contact with relatives. A girl in Harare commented of her employers,

> When my relatives come, they do not welcome them or greet them properly... They do not want me to use their telephone. When my relatives phone, they do not want me to speak with them.

Some employers do not give the children adequate time to visit their relatives, even in cases of emergency. A 16-year-old girl complained:

> My father has a bad leg. He broke his leg and has no one to help him with money. I heard this from my mother's sister, but I have not yet gone to see him because I have not been given time to go home.

Children on their own can easily be lonely. One girl complained specifically that her employer showed no sympathy when she was sad. Children sometimes had difficulty in contacting peers and finding company. Some child employees commented that they were not allowed to chat with neighbouring children, and were discouraged generally from talking to outsiders. When asked if friends ever visited them at their place of work, many of the children replied that their employers did not allow such visits. In order to ensure the social and psychological development of the child, employers should ensure that the children have regular and suitable company. This applies even to children in more customary rural settings: it was important for Temba that his friends came to play with him on Sundays.

Working for kin

A number of the case studies we have cited show children being helped by relatives in exchange for services. This kind of co-operation between kin fits easily into traditional ideals of solidarity and support with extended families. Children working for kin are more likely to be happy in their work than children working for employers who are unknown to their families. But there can be problems with working for kin. Indeed the best scenario appears to be children working for an unrelated family acquaintance, with regular visits from their family (17 out of 21 in this situation said they were happy in their work).

One of the problems with working for kin is that the work is seen as a cultural obligation of children towards their seniors, rather than as a contractual exchange. In the case of Tawanda and his sister, Tawanda was employed by acquaintances from church and was paid for his work, while his sister helped his aunt and was not paid. When working for kin, there is no clear delineation of duties.

Danny (see above) was taken on to garden for his uncle when his father died. He was happy about the way his uncle and aunt treated him. They respected that he had come with his mother who had presented them with a problem, and he had shown a willingness to work in order to improve his situation. Initially, however, there were problems from the children of the family:

> They would throw stones at me, scolding me that I should
> go back home as I had come to finish their food.

Danny went to school in the morning and worked in the afternoon. During weekends and school holidays he worked for four hours in the morning. His tasks included the general maintenance of the garden and the yard, and washing the car. Sometimes he was given extra tasks, and he commented,

> Since I work for my uncle I would do whatever he tells me
> to do, because he might think that I am challenging him.

He said that if he was working for someone who was not his relative, he would ask for extra pay if the tasks were so divorced from his day-to-day duties.

Danny recalled a time when he was burning dried grass, which led to a hedge catching fire. His uncle called in his mother, who apologised for the accident. When she left, his uncle beat him. Danny commented,

> I was so angry that I just walked out wandering aimlessly.
> I did not know what to do because I thought my mother
> had resolved the issue, so I could not go home and tell her
> I didn't want to work anymore.

There is always a danger of children being coerced to work for kin, and of being coerced by kin to do extra work. While working for kin can be satisfactory way of being socialised into responsibilities to one's family, it can also deteriorate into a form of forced labour, which is condemned internationally.

Contracts

Danny mentioned extra tasks being given him by his uncle, and we saw in the case of Nomsa how tasks could be accumulated. In the case of adult domestic workers, a written contract is required by law. Few of the children (30 percent) had formal contracts of employment, and the children have pointed to this as a problem in workshops and meetings. We notice that children with formal contracts were more likely to be content in their work than those without.[66]

A contract would specify hours and kinds of work required of the children, as well as times off and various benefits. The danger is that employers regard children as 'family' not in need of anything so formal. In practice, this means that the children are at the call of the employers all day, and even at night, seven days a week. We shall be looking at complaints by some children of the long hours they are made to work.

Some international commentaries of child domestic work point out that the way to avoid children being badly exploited, is for the work to be recognised as employment, and not to be simply considered as 'helping out' in exchange for keep.[67] In this way, tasks, hours, and appropriate remuneration can be clearly agreed. Such formality does not mean that the relationship should be impersonal. As we shall see, child workers also like to be treated as members of the family.

A formal contract would not guarantee that children will be able to enforce its terms. More important than the formality is a clear agreement about the responsibilities of the worker. If extra work occasionally arises, there should be agreement on the part of the worker to take on the extra work, and agreement as to how the worker should be compensated.

Education

The right of children to education is asserted in both the United Nations Convention and the African Charter. Both documents assert that children should be able to progress in their education according to their ability. It is also the policy of Save the Children that working children should be able to combine their work with suitable education.[68] People usually think of education as formal schooling, but this is not the only form of education and not necessarily the most useful for children in families that are struggling for their livelihood. The Movement for Working Children is more specific about what they consider to be their rights: they have a right to learn to read and write and the right to learn a trade.

> We should not only go to school, but school should also
> come to us, in order to learn more...[69]

Child domestic workers in Senegal have been happy with training towards a formal certificate specifically related to domestic work, which would improve their recognition and status.[70] They need a system of education that fits their needs.

Many people assume that employment conflicts with education. More detailed studies show that it is poverty rather than work that relates to poor school performance.[71] Employment sometimes brings benefits, training children in handling money and in responsibility.[72] Among communities in which there is economic hardship, employment may be necessary for the children's livelihood. The basic needs of food, clothing, and shelter must be met before education becomes possible. In poor communities, it is often precisely employment that makes education possible, by paying for the costs of education.[73] In the hyper-inflationary economy of Zimbabwe, these costs are increasingly falling outside the means of families, without some input from children's incomes. Employers, who are responsible for the well-being of their child employees, have some responsibility to see that their right to education is fulfilled – although this becomes increasingly difficult as costs of education soar.

Our case studies show education to be a high priority in the children's minds. Where domestic work makes the child's education and further training possible, this is a benefit for the child.

A 17-year-old girl works around 6 hours a day, and her employer pays her fees for secondary school. She likes her work, likes receiving her pay, and likes having her schooling paid for. She does not like the way the employers' children insult her. But she does not want to stop working.

> If I stop, I would not find money for school and would be a trouble to my mother.

A 14-year-old boy commented,

> If I stop, there is no way I could pay for school.

A 17-year-old boy explained more fully.

> Where I work, they treat me well because they give me the money I need for school if I fail to find my share. But if I could find money for school, I would prefer not to work. One of my parents died, the one who provided the money I needed for school, and that is why I am working. But I say to other children who are not going to school, 'Look for what you can do to find money that will enable you to go to school.'

Another girl commented:

> If ZDAWU would speak for us to Social Welfare to pay our fees at school, so that we study and pass, then I could work for the books. I wish ZDAWU could cover shoes and uniforms for school, because the money I earn is not enough.

Some employers are conscientious and helpful in the matter of education. Of the children who managed to continue their schooling, ten (out of 37) had their fees paid by their employers.[74] Three of these were working for relatives, and two, for people previously known to the parents: five employers, although previously unknown to the child's family, ensured that the child they employed was educated. More significantly, eight of these were in Zvishavane – the small-town culture tends to care better for working children, than does the drive of big cities.

While employment sometimes makes education possible, it can still interfere with school performance. A 17-year-old boy commented in detail.

> I work for my *sekuru* [75] but the reason for this is poverty. I say that if my father was able to find enough money to send me to school, I would be a person who does better at school, because I would have time to read well and do homework and relax my legs and be in our own house. Now things concerning work are tedious because someone is watching to see that you do the work, as if you are prostituting yourself. The things of school are considered a favour, as if you entered work without the aim of being sent to school.

Education needs attention among our child domestic workers. At workshops, children have pointed out that education is the most important benefit that they should be getting from their work. Of our sample, 33 (25 percent) had not completed their primary education[76] and of these only 16 were still in school.[77] Five of the children admitted to never having been to school. Only half had reached secondary school.[78]

Only 37 of the children, or just over a quarter of our sample, were still in school.[79] In only one case, the child was doing a training course, apart from formal schooling. This was a 16-year-old boy who had completed form four and was being helped by his elder brother to do a sewing course in his spare time (in the cross-tabulation tables, we have counted him among those still at school). We notice, not surprisingly, that the majority of those who were still in school were also content in their work.[80]

Of the children who were not in school, the majority (86 percent) were in the older age group – above 15. While only 14 percent of this group were still in school, the figure rose to 61 percent for the younger children below 15 (still a low figure).[81] The vast majority of those out of school (over 90 percent) cited lack of funds as the reason for leaving school.[82] One claimed that work left no time for school. Two had completed their schooling, and one refused to continue at school (having reached grade 5). Other reasons could also have been related to lack of money, such as,

> My father, who was sending me to school, died.

At a workshop in Harare in September 2001, child domestic workers put as one of their top priorities to negotiate with employers for time to go back to school.

Recommendations

We recommend the following, when arrangements are being made to employ a child domestic worker.

• Both the child and the guardians must be willing partners and agree to the arrangement.

• Care should be taken to ensure that the child is free to leave, if he or she becomes dissatisfied with the arrangement, and that extra work and overtime, are not imposed on the child without the child's full agreement and outside the prescribed limit of hours of work.

• A formal contract should be drawn up, indicating responsibilities, hours of work, holidays and other benefits, terms of payment, and any other agreements relevant to the employment. There should be a national format for such contracts, which should indicate penalties for the breach of specific clauses.

• Such a contract should be drawn up even when the child is working for kin.

• The contract should state what provisions are being made for the child's continued education or training as well as the responsibility of the employer in this respect.

• Guardians should ensure that a relative or someone trusted by the child visits him or her regularly at the place of work. Employers must respect the right of children to retain contact with their families.

• When the child is living far from home, employers should ensure that he or she has adequate opportunity to visit their family regularly.

NOTES

58. *Statutory Instrument* 155 of 1999.

59. See *Statutory Instrument* 72 of 1997.

60 Table 5.

61 ILO Convention no. 182, article 3 (a).

62. Table 9.

63. Table 11. Notice that with a chi-squared probability of .24, the relationship between being happy and being within walking distance of the previous home is not proven.

64. Table 10.

65. Table 11.

66. Table 13.

67. See UNICEF, *Child Domestic Work*, p. 15.

68. Save the Children, *Children and Work: Save the Children's position on children and work* (London, Save the Children, 2003), p. 12.

69. African Movement of Working Children and Youth, *'A world fit for and by children': Our Point of View as African Working Children* (Dakar, ENDA Tiers-Monde, 2001), p. 8.

70. Pierre Marie Coulibaly and Dibou Faye, *Le programme AEJT* – ENDA – Gouvernement – IPEC/BIT au Sénégal (Report from ENDA Tiers-Monde, Dakar, 1999).

71. See Myers, 'Can children's work and education be reconciled?' pp. 308-309.

72. See Michael Bourdillon, 'Translating standards into practice: confronting local barriers', in *Child Labor and Human Rights: Making Children Matter* (ed.) Burns Weston (Boulder, Lynne Reiner, 2005), pp.143-166.

73. See Michael Bourdillon, 'Child labour and education: a case study from south-eastern Zimbabwe', *Journal of Social Development in Africa* 15 (2000), 2, pp. 5-32.

74. Table 17.

75. This term refers to a number of relatives, either of the grandparents generation, or a man of one's mother's lineage.

76. Table 14

77. Table 16.

78. Table 14.

79. Table 15.

80. Table 18.

81. Table 19.

82. Table 20.

6

Conditions of Work

Complaints

At the same workshop for working children in September of 2001, the child domestic workers mentioned five problem areas; low pay; physical and sexual abuse; being required to wash the underwear of employers; inadequate or no leave; and not being allowed to enjoy facilities such as television. At a national workshop for working children in August 2003, child domestic workers complained of long hours starting early in the morning and finishing late at night, as well as no time off.

Hours of work

The *Labour Relations (Employment of Children and Young Persons) Regulation* of 1997 stipulated that children aged from 12 to 17 may be employed in 'light work', which is defined as not more than six hours in any one day. They are entitled to one and a half days off per week, of which at least 24 hours must be continuous.[83] As we have pointed out, these regulations were amended in 1999, when the minimum age of employment was raised to 15. While strict enforcement of the legislation would result in some children losing their access to income for livelihood and for education, it is a matter of concern that many children are being required to work for hours that substantially exceed those allowed, and that some very young children are employed.

We asked the children in the survey to list the tasks they performed during the day and to estimate the time spent on each. Many were unable to do this in a manner that we found convincing, and the figures that we do have are probably not accurate in many cases. In some cases, we guessed the hours spent from their descriptions of jobs. We counted all duties as work. If the child employer had to escort young children to and from school, the work is not heavy, but it is still time that the child cannot spend in any other way.

The children's responses showed the wide variation in treatment that working children receive, and indicate that some children are being badly exploited.[84] Only a third of the children (32 percent) worked for six hours a day or less. Nearly half of those we recorded (44 percent) were working for more than eight hours a day, the normal maximum allowed for adults. Although the majority of those still in school had light work loads, this was not always the case.[85] Ten (30 percent) of those in school were working six or more hours a day and five were working over eight hours a day, apart from their schoolwork. One child listed as the first thing he disliked about his work,

> Not finding time to read, or even the time for school… I do
> not find time for schoolwork.

We discussed hours of work with a group in Gweru. Although they knew that children under fifteen are not by law supposed to work in employment for more than six hours a day, they felt that this was unrealistic. Based on their own experiences, they proposed a maximum of six hours a day for children under 13, eight hours a day for children in the 13 to 14 age group, and ten hours a day for children aged from 15 to 17.

We asked the children whether they get time off to rest and nearly half (43 percent) said that they did not.[87] One commented that she was only able to rest when the employers were out. In their complaints about the way their employers treat them , seven complained at the amount of work they had to do (one commenting that there was no time to rest), one complained of no time for schoolwork, one complained of not being allowed to play, and one complained of no time to talk to others. Over half said that they do not have a chance to play with other children.[88]

Adult domestic workers are required by law to have one and a half days off a week, of which one day must be 24 hours continuously. Forty-four of our sample (31 percent) said that they did not get days off,[89] while others commented that they get only Sunday off. One child complained that even on her off days, she was given chores to do before she was allowed to go. Forty-nine, or 34 percent of the sample, claimed that they were not allowed to be off duty on public holidays. Some of the children were allowed to accumulate their days off in order to take four days off together to visit their families. Besides regular days off, adult domestic workers are required by law to have thirty days of leave a year, and up to twelve days of occasional leave for specified emergencies. Over half the children claimed that they did not get leave.[90] Another pointed out that no one did any cleaning while she was away, so that when she came back she had a backlog of cleaning to do.

Apart from the number of hours they do, in some cases there is a problem of the times that the children are required to work, interfering with their sleep. While medical knowledge is uncertain on the hours of sleep needed by children, the general consensus is that older children need around eight hours of sleep at night.[91] When asked what they do not like about their work, two of our sample complained of getting up early, two of going to bed late, while four complained of both of these. Five others commented that they had no time to rest. One girl pointed out that she was first up in the house and last to bed and when the employers retired, they sometimes gave her further chores to do before she went to bed. Another 15-year-old girl commented,

> How can I be happy when I am woken at four and go to bed
> at ten at night and all the work is for me to do?

The early rising to prepare breakfast and get children ready for school, comprise an essential component of the work for which many children are employed. Employers may say that the children do not in fact work such long hours, and are often idle during the day when the employer is away at work. As we shall see, the working children sometimes comment on the fact that they are only able to rest when the employer is out. Employers may also argue that going to bed late may be due to watching television instead of doing their chores. Some children, however, are not allowed to relax in the lounge and watch television. An employer who takes on the responsibility of looking after a live-in child domestic worker, should see that the child has adequate time to rest and to sleep.

Occasionally a teenage child worker is given the task of caring for an elderly or sick person, perhaps sharing the room of the elderly person in order to be able to provide help if needed during the night (as we saw in the case of Nomsa). Although the relationship that develops while caring for an elderly person can be a rewarding experience and is appreciated by the child, employers still have an obligation to see that the child gets adequate rest. Work done at night should be compensated for by time off during the day.

Because they are children, frequently doing chores that children are expected to do, employers often do not see the need to give them specified times of work and free time to relax with their friends.

Payment

At the time of the survey, the legal minimum wage for an adult domestic worker was $13,060[92] (or $15,800 for a child minder). This minimum wage is notorious for falling behind inflation. The wages children are paid vary greatly and are not always comparable. A child who works part-time while still at school, can expect to earn less than an older child who is doing full-time work. On the other hand, some of the children are paid very little for long hours of work. One child was being paid $1,500 a month and was expected to work around eight hours a day. Several of the children were being paid $2,000 or $2,500 a month for a full day's work. In one extreme case, a sixteen-year-old girl was receiving $2,500 and her duties took up around 15 hours a day. It is difficult to make fixed recommendations about wages in a highly inflationary economy, other than they should relate to the cost of living. It is clear that some of the children were being both over-worked and under-paid.

Several of the children complained of being short-paid, or having money deducted when they make a mistake (this may be to replace items that they have broken). The employer has no right to deduct moneys from an agreed wage without proper procedures being followed.

Kundai (see above), said of her second employer,

> She gave me a jacket one day when it was very cold, she did not say whether it was being sold I thought she was being kind. When I asked for my pay long after month-end, I was told, 'We are deducting money for the jacket.'

Of another occasion, Kundai had this to say:

> I burnt her skirt by error one day when I was ironing and when I showed her the skirt, she was so angry she threw the skirt to my face and said she did not want the skirt. She wanted a skirt with no burnt marks. She threatened that she was going to deduct money from my wages to buy her

expensive skirt.

Whether she deducted the money or not made no difference, as Kundai rarely received the pay due to her. The employer claimed she was giving the pay to Kundai's grandmother, but her grandmother denied this.

From our sample, in 19 cases[93] (14 percent), the wages were given to a guardian and not to the child. As the children have pointed out, the child is the one who works and therefore it is important for him or her to be given the payment. They say that sometimes when the child goes home and shows the money they have earned to their parents, the parents simply take their money. Apart from the fact that children, like anyone else, should receive benefits from the work they do, there is a danger that they can become unwilling providers of services for the benefit of their 'guardians'.

Nevertheless some children approve of such arrangements, or at least saw advantages as well as disadvantages.

Brilliant's employer gave his wages directly to his grandfather, who had made the arrangements for his employment. In turn the grandfather made sure that school fees are paid on time, and that Brilliant was fed and clothed. Grandfather took care of his welfare, as well as that of his brother and cousins. Brilliant was not happy with the kind of clothes that his grandfather bought for him

> because grandfather buys clothes that are not fashionable. I want to buy the side pockets, which other children are wearing, but he always says those clothes are not strong.

But he also said that it was good that his employer gave the money to his grandfather because

> my friends might influence me badly and I would end up with no money for school fees or even assist my grandparents with the welfare of the family. That arrangement though I don't get to see my money its ok, because in a way they are protecting me. If my friends know that I have got money or that I get money at the end of the month they may influence me to drink.

Brilliant did not even know how much he was now paid.

> It doesn't matter how much I get because the fees and the clothes I get are more than my pay. Things are

now expensive.

His employers also sometimes gave him gifts like second hand clothes. He attributed this to his hard working and obedience and said,

> I think it shows that they are happy with the work that I do.

Over a third of our sample (35 percent) claimed that they were often not paid at the month's end, when their wages became due. In several cases, officers of ZDAWU were asked to approach employers to extract what is due. Some children claimed that their employers sometimes borrow money from them when their wages become due. The children are in a subordinate position and find it hard to claim back their wages when employers use their money for other things, even if it is intended to be temporary.

At workshops, children have made many points about the payment of wages to child domestic workers. These all arise from unhappy experiences.

• The wages should be agreed with the children and must be enough to cover necessities.

• Payments should be on time, on a specified day at the end of the month.

• Payments must include cash wages. Children should not be expected to work only for their keep. Also it is not good enough to pay them only in kind, such as in second-hand clothing.

• The wages should be paid to the children and not to one or more guardians.

• Pay should not be borrowed by the employer.

Kinds of work

The children say that young children are sometimes given jobs that are not appropriate for their age and that work should be graded according to age.

Some complaints by children suggested a lack of sensitivity to their feelings. A 17-year-old boy complained at having to bathe girl children. There were several complaints about having to wash other people's underwear by hand, something that is not acceptable in traditional culture. A 17-year-old girl commented:

> The people I work for treat me badly. The mother and the
> father I work for are cruel. The mother tells me to wash
> her underwear and her husband's, but I am not happy. She
> also tells me to make the bed.

A 16-year old girl working in Harare commented that the worst thing about her job was washing her employer's bed linen after she had been sleeping with her boyfriend.

More generally, children sometimes complain at being given work that they perceive not to be appropriate to their gender. When asked to indicate things that they liked and things that they disliked about their work, several boys mentioned that they disliked cooking, sweeping, and tidying the house, whereas these jobs were often mentioned as tasks that girls liked. Girls on the other hand disliked having to work in the garden or washing the car, tasks that boys liked. Some tasks, such as washing laundry and plates, were disliked by both girls and boys.

In discussion with groups of child domestic workers, the children pointed out that what they think is reasonable differs from what they are expected to do in practice. They also notice that some children are more competent than others at certain tasks and it is difficult to set definite rules about what children can do at particular ages. Although the children in our discussions were older than twelve, some had started working in employment when they were younger, and remembered how difficult it was to cope with the work and responsibility when they were so young.

The groups decided that young children under the age of 13 should be expected to do only the simplest of tasks, like sweeping and washing dishes. They can do their own laundry, but should not be expected to do that of the whole house. They can do other chores that can be fun with other children, like washing cars.

The groups agreed that children aged 13 to 14 can wash plates, cook, wash clothes (but point out that it is against custom to wash other people's underwear), and iron clothes. They learn these things from a young age. They should not be expected to work in the garden. They should not be expected to handle poisonous chemicals, such as those to kill cockroaches in the house or pests in the garden - young people do not understand how harmful these things can be. They should not be expected to handle money.

Children under 15 should not be required to carry heavy loads, since their bodies have not yet built up. We noticed that some children complained at the strain of putting heavy goods on a cart, while others quite liked carrying loads when they earned extra money in this way. The environment affected the way children perceived what was reasonable. The point remains, the loads carried should be appropriate to the child's physical strength.

Children aged 15-17 can work in the garden, though some girls felt that this was unsuitable for them. They can be sent to sell things and manage a stall, because they have learned the value of money and can handle change. They can be sent on errands, but should not be sent on errands at night, when they can be molested and even robbed.

We are concerned that children, even young children, are left to look after the home while adults are away, sometimes with even younger children of the household present in their care. We asked the child domestic workers if they are ever left alone with the children of the house. Some pointed out that there are no children where they work. Over a third (38 percent) said that they do spend time alone with the children, and escorting young children to school or the crèche is a common task for the workers.[94] This applies to children of all ages, although some commented that they spend time playing with the other children, and it is not clear that the positive answers mean that the worker is in charge of other children, or whether there is an adult present who can be easily called.

In discussion, children suggested that young children under 13 can be left play with toddlers, provided there is an adult around, but they should not be expected to take care of children in the absence of adults. Older children can take care of younger ones, and those aged 15-17 can even take care of babies for half a day. The children say that they do not have the experience of a mother, and cannot provide the same kind of care that mothers can give - if they are left for longer, accidents can happen.

We also asked if they were ever left alone in the house. Ten (29 percent) of the younger age groups answered positively, as did 65 percent of the older group.[95] Most of the responses indicated that they were alone in the house while the owners were away at work during the day, on weekdays. In a couple of cases, when something went wrong during the day, children mentioned being helped by neighbours. Five of the older workers (in the 15-18 age group) mentioned that they sometimes stay in the house when the owners are away overnight (in the case of one fifteen-year-old girl, for up to three days).

The point was made at a workshop that it was too heavy a responsibility for a child to look after a home with no adults present. In the group discussions, children pointed out that con-artists may visit the house during the day, and younger children may believe them, so they say that no one under 15 should be left alone in charge of the house. Older children can look after the house during the day, but they should not be left alone overnight. They will be blamed if thieves come and rob the house, yet there is nothing they can do.

Working environment

We asked the children if they were happy with the way their employers treat them. Only a third of them replied positively.[96] Among those that were not happy (87 cases), the most common explanation was the way they are insulted and shouted at (29 cases). Five mentioned being beaten. Related to this, 20 children complained that they were generally not treated well; they were not treated like a person; they were treated like someone bad; or 'like a slave'; or like someone who does not think; or a person without parents of their own. One girl said graphically of her employer,

> He thinks I work like the engine of a motorcar, but I have blood.

A 17-year-old girl complained that the employer did not want her to talk with the children of the house. Some employers discourage their children from any familiarity with child workers. Some child workers complained that they were not allowed to watch television or sit on a sofa in the lounge. One commented that if she drank from a cup that the employers used, it would be thrown away.

Fifty-four children (40 percent) believed that the employers were not satisfied with their performance.[97] The reason for this was usually the way the employers scolded them. Another 23 had no idea whether their employers were satisfied or not. It would help to overcome the low self-esteem often found in child domestic workers, if employers expressed their appreciation to children who do a job well. One girl explicitly complained that people do not see the work she does.

Some children have complained that employers pay insufficient attention to health and safety. Protective clothing is not always supplied where it is needed such as boots and gloves for certain kinds of garden work. More particularly, children are not always shown how to use electrical and other equipment safely. We asked the children if they were taught how to use equipment, and 43 replied that they had not been taught.[98]

Lack of respect

We have mentioned that children have a right to respect and dignity. We have also mentioned the world-wide hazard of child domestic workers losing self esteem, which often results from lack of respect. We tend to look down on people who are not as well off as ourselves. When children are poor and have to work for their livelihood, it is easy to treat them as inferior. Equally, it is easy to look down on children who have lost their parents and have no one to look after them, although there is no logical reason why this should be so. Urban people often feel superior to rural people, and so are especially likely to look down on children from rural areas. Lack of respect is a major problem for child domestic workers.

The children's most common complaint was that they were constantly being scolded, an issue that came up repeatedly in what the children do not like about work. The Shona word for this, *kutukwa*, is sometimes translated as 'to be shouted at' and it carries heavy connotations of insult. The children were complaining of lack of respect. In practice, around half of the children were treated with angry and insulting scolding; some were beaten; a few had money deducted from their wages; and some were even deprived of food.[99] Such treatment arises from the fact that they are being treated as children, perhaps even as 'family', rather than as employees with rights.

One of the areas of strong complaint from the children is the way they are treated when they make mistakes. One child pointed out that it would better if when they make a mistake they are corrected without shouting. Children have the right to be treated with respect and when they make mistakes, they can be advised so politely.

This is partly a problem of respecting children and their rights generally. In Zimbabwe, as in many countries throughout the world, children are often treated with scant respect and ignored as if they have no opinions worth hearing. The problem is exacerbated, however, when the children are of a lower socio-economic class than are the relevant adults. Indeed, occasionally children complained of being insulted and even beaten by other children of the household.

Culturally, children receive the status due to their families, and particularly their parents. Parents and the family are expected to take care of them and to seek redress against anyone who treats their children badly. When parents and family are not around, there is no adult to demand that the children have status and are treated with respect. We saw in the case of Tariro how even a relative made no effort to fulfil her obligation to educate her employee until her family came to visit and complain.

When we come across a child who has lost his or her parents, or who for other reasons is without family support to speak up for them, it is easy to forget they are people who think and feel like other children. The children themselves sometimes complain of being treated like orphans; they have taken up this cultural reaction that children without parents are to be despised.

While the issue of respect applies particularly to the employers and their families, it also has broader application. A 15-year-old boy commented:

> For my part, I work well, and accordingly some people give me respect because I am on the road forwards, but others despise me and laugh at me. I do not mind because my affairs go well.

In the present situation in Zimbabwe, when children are living away from home, and particularly when they are learning to cope without their parents, they show enterprise and initiative. They should be respected in their own right, for who they are and for what they are doing for themselves.

Fears of child workers

One of the criteria for work to be classified among the worst forms of child labour is that it is hazardous – if by the circumstances in which it is carried out, it is likely to harm the health or safety of the child.[100] We asked the children if they had ever felt they were in danger at work. Over a third replied in the affirmative.[101] The most common source of danger was electricity (13 cases), especially from cookers. Ten cases referred to work in the garden; spraying vegetables without gloves (6 cases); operating a lawn mower without boots; chopping wood; and getting sap in the eyes when cutting the hedge. Three felt in danger when having to clean the toilet without gloves and three more from washing underwear, or dirty children's clothes.

One girl felt she was in danger 'sometimes when I sleep because I am not allowed to sleep during the day'. While this danger would fall away if the child obeyed the rules of her employer, there is often a serious problem of inadequate hours of sleep for the children. Three others commented that the danger they felt arose from the fact that they had too much work and not enough sleep.

Two complained that they felt danger because they did not get enough to eat, one commenting that he could not do his work properly. Four were afraid of being scolded and insulted, one commenting that he made mistakes from having so much to do.

Some dangers arose from living conditions. One said he was very cold at night. Two felt in danger of getting burnt at night. One felt danger at having to go to the toilet in the dark. A 12-year-old girl felt she was in danger when she was washing, which she had to do behind the house.

Outside our sample, children have complained of danger from thieves or thugs when sent on errands, especially at night. One child in our sample mentioned that he did not like having to run errands outside the house at night.

Less than a quarter of the children (31 of them) said that they had suffered an accident at work. Four of these referred to incidents that got them into trouble with employers, while another referred to a problem with the employer not returning his money, accusing him of theft. Eight had received electric shocks and four had been burned or scalded. When medical treatment was required, employers helped to obtain this. One boy lost some money, a fourteen-year-old girl felt in danger when she was selling for her employer and made a mistake in the change - the girl buying from her beat her.

It is important to be aware of the dangers of electrical equipment and make sure that children who are not familiar with such equipment are made thoroughly aware of how to deal with electricity safely. Perhaps a problem here is that the employers themselves are not always aware of the potential dangers of electrical gadgets.

Recommendations

• Children must be treated with respect. Even when correction is needed, this should be administered in a way that does not remove the child's human dignity.

• Employers should make a conscious effort to ensure that their child employees do not lose their self esteem. Children should be given clear encouragement when they work well.

• The hours of work should be moderate and relate to the age of the child, their need for time for schooling and to the pay they receive.

• Children should get adequate time to sleep.Employers of live-in working children act as their guardians and are responsible for seeing that the employee gets the hours of rest appropriate to their age. Children under 13 should normally have nine hours of sleep per night, children aged 13 to 14 should have 8 1/2 hours, while children aged 15 to 17 should have 8 hours.

• Wages should be related to inflation, and ensure that the children can buy what they need, with something to spare either for their families, or to save.

• The work and responsibilities given to the children should be appropriate for their ages. In particular;

> – Young children under 13 can only be expected to do simple chores, like sweeping and washing dishes. They should not be expected to do the laundry for the whole household. They should not be left alone with younger children (although they can play with toddlers when

there is an adult around).

- Children under 15 should not work with poisonous chemicals.

- Children under 15 should not be required to do heavy gardening work

- Children under 15 should not be expected to handle money.

- Children under 15 should not be left alone in the house, and should not be left alone in charge of younger children.

- Children under 18 should not be left alone in the house overnight.

- Children under 18 should not be left to care for babies for more than half a day.

- Children under 18 should not be sent on errands at night.

• The children should be carefully instructed on safety procedures with respect to any equipment they use.

• Children should be provided with appropriate protective clothing when liable to come into contact with harmful substances, such as chemicals or refuse.

• Children should not be sent on errands that jeopardise their safety.

• Children should receive compensation for injuries arising out of their work.

NOTES

83. Statutory Instrument 72 of 1997.

84. Table 21.

85. Table 22

86. Table 23.

87. See Table 30.

88. Table 24.

89. Table 25.

90. Table 26.

91. A study on children aged 11 to 14 in Chicago, showed significant increases in rates of depression, low self esteem, and low grades, when average hours of sleep dropped from eight hours a night to seven. Katia Fredriksen, Jean Rhodes, Ranjini Reddy, and Niobe Way, 'Sleepless in Chicago: Tracking the effects of adolescent sleep loss during middle school years', *Child Development* 75 (2004), 1, pp. 84–95.

92. At that time, the official exchange rate was around Z$800 to US$1. The black market rate was around Z$5,000 to US$1. A realistic purchasing value is somewhere in between, nearer to the official rate for basic commodities produced locally, and close to the black market rate for imported goods.

93. We could find nothing significant about these 19 cases. Nine were in the younger age groups; 12 were happy in their work; only five claimed that they were forced to work; seven were still in school. The only variable that differed significantly from the rest of the children was that the majority (12) were visited by relatives We conclude that children are often happy to work for the benefit of their families.

94. Table 27.

95. Table 28.

96. Table 30.

97. Table 31.

98. Table 32

99. Table 29.

100. ILO Convention 182, article 3 (d).

101. Table 33

102. Table 34.

7

Living Conditions

Two thirds of the child workers live with their employers.[103] Of these, around half (52 percent) sleep in a bedroom in the house, usually like one of the family.[104] In the case of Nomsa, the child was called in from an outhouse to stay in the bedroom of an old lady she had to care for. While her living conditions improved, her workload also increased. as she was constantly having to do things for the patient, even during the night.

Living in can have advantages for the child, providing better conditions than they might have at home. A 15-year-old boy commented that he would like to find a situation where:

> I would work, living at the place of work and going to school and not going to work and then going back to our home.

Forty-three percent of the live-in workers sleep in the kitchen or dining area. In some cases, this is simply due to crowded living conditions, and the employee may be sleeping in the living area together with children of the household. Often the sleeping conditions of the workers are clearly distinct from those of children of the household. In a few cases, children complained of the cold, or of the danger of being burnt by the fire while trying to keep warm at night.

Sleeping in the public space can seem good to the child. Brilliant used to sleep in the dining-room at his employers' house when he first started working. Then his employers built a shed where gardening equipment was kept and where there was room for Brilliant to sleep with privacy. Brilliant was, however, upset with the idea that he should be sleeping in the shed with his tools and preferred after that, to go home to his grandfather's house every night

Feeding arrangements sometimes give rise to tensions between the child workers and their employers. At one workshop, children pointed out that you can starve when living with the employer, if you are only receiving money, since you may not have enough money to buy food when you need to. When the child is living with the employers, the provision of meals is important to the child's well-being and happiness. We asked the children about their eating arrangements and whether they had comments on the food. Around half ate with the family for whom they worked and another quarter were given the same food, although they ate separately.[105] Some explained that they ate separately because they were not members of the family.

Only three of the 38 who were given different food from what their employers eat said that they were happy in their work.[106] Fourteen complained that they were not given enough to eat and six commented that they ate from what was left, when the others had all eaten. One commented,

> Me, I am given food ... the meat is no different from what they give their dog.

Another said,

> I see that the food that I am given is not enough for the kind of work I do, because there is much work so that you remain unsatisfied, but they want their work done.

A girl in a Harare suburb (earning $5,000 a month) complained she has no money to buy things. When she broke a plate, money was deducted from her wages.

> My food in this place is sadza only. For tea they say, 'Buy sugar with your own money.' So this means that I work only to eat.

Another girl commented of her employers,

> They do not want me to use their things, not even to drink water from their cup... They say, 'Don't even taste my food or eat my food.' If they leave any food uneaten, they give it to the dog. If I suggest that I might eat the food they have left, they say, 'You are not my relative.'

Here we see the status of the child being denigrated to an extreme. Some employers explicitly separate child employees from their families. The employees are forbidden use of the family's recreational facilities and live and eat apart. We saw in the case of Nomsa how she regarded her situation as improving when she moved into the family house, in spite of the extra work it involved. On the other hand, other children said in appreciation of their employers that they were treated as one of the family, or as the employer's own child.[107]

Children sometimes appreciate the situation of child domestic workers and behave differently when their parents are away. One boy said his happiest times at work are when both his employers, husband and wife, were out of the house; then their daughter lets him in the house to watch videotapes.

An area of concern is what happens to child workers when they are sick. We asked the children if they had ever been sick while they were at work and if so, who looked after them.[108] Less than a third of them were cared for by their employers or by members of the employers' households. Sixteen who were sick said that no one helped them and they got better on their own, sometimes explicitly mentioning that they had bought medicines. Another child said that no one helped her with money, but the people she worked for brought water to cool her down. Children point out that the wages they earn are not usually enough for medicines.

Children have also complained that sometimes their employers do not believe them when they say they are not feeling well and force them to go on working. Alternatively, some employers do not allow the children time off, and suggest that instead they should do only light work while they are not well. Some employers deduct wages for the time that the children are sick and not working. We that one of the twelve rights of children emphasised by the African Movement of Working Children and Youth, is the right to rest when they are sick.

We have seen that few of the children were happy with the way their employers treated them. About half (47 percent) were happy with the way the rest of the family treated them.[109] In seven cases, the children were happy with the way their employer treated them, but not with the way they were treated by other members of the family. Again, the common complaint was the way people scolded and insulted them (13 cases) or beat them (5 cases). In some cases, other children treated the workers badly in the absence of adults. One child who was working for his aunt complained that the older boys in the house beat him when his aunt was away. We noticed that when Danny started working for his uncle, his cousins did not welcome his presence.

There were complaints about being laughed at; being loathed; not being deemed worth talking to; not being treated as a person; not being treated as a person with relatives or parents; or as a slave or prisoner; or that members of the house do not respect a worker. Related to this were complaints about not being allowed access to the facilities of the house – to television, to sitting on the sofa, and even in one case not being allowed to use utensils that the householders use. A 15-year-old girl complained, 'Mwana wavo anonditarira zvikuru.' [Their child stares at me.] Apart from employers treating child workers with respect (as we have discussed in relation to working conditions), there is need to ensure that other members of the household also treat child workers with the respect owing to all people.

We asked the children if they were allowed to leave the house in which they work. The majority (82 children or 57 percent) replied that they were not. It is not clear how strictly this rule was enforced or in what circumstances. Virtually all our respondents were able to attend meetings of working children. Particularly in the case of younger children, the employers have a responsibility of seeing that they come to no harm, which means that the adults must exercise some control over the children's movements. Nevertheless, the comments of the children on their relations with children of the household make clear their need for recreation and for the social company of their peers.

Recommendations

• Children who live in should be provided with adequate accommodation, ensuring adequate sleep.

• Children should receive adequate food while at work. Employers are responsible to see that this is the case if the child is living at the place of work.

• When a child is living at the place of work, employers are responsible to see that he or she receives care when they are sick. Medical insurance is recommended, without which the employer should cover the costs of necessary medicines. In any case, the issue of responsibility in case the child becomes sick, should be agreed when initial arrangements are made.

• Employers should ensure that the child worker is treated with respect by all members of the household.

• Especially in the case of young workers, it helps when, as far as possible, they are treated as part of the family. Such treatment should be combined with a clear statement of the child's duties and payments.

NOTES

103. Table 35.

104. Table 36.

105. Table 37.

106. Table 38.

107. In her study of child domestic workers in Abidjan, Mélanie Jacquemin points out that being treated as family was a key to the child's contentment. 'Children's domestic work in Abidjan, Côte d'Ivoire: The *petites bonnes* have the floor', *Childhood* 11 (2004), 3, p. 393. See also Sommerfelt, *Domestic Child Labour in Morocco*, p. 33.

108. Table 39 and Table 40. We notice that costs of treatment often became contentious between employers of child domestic workers in Morocco and the children's families: Sommerfelt, *Domestic Child Labour in Morocco*, p. 37.

109. Table 41

8

Abuse

Working children are vulnerable to abuse, especially if there are no family members in the vicinity to see that they are being treated well. The children in our sample are working for employers who did not stop them from attending meetings of working children. In spite of this bias towards children under employers who give them some space, we have seen that some are physically beaten and many are shouted at and complain of lack of respect from employers and their families. We have seen that some of the children are not given adequate time to visit their families. Even allowing for the possibility of some exaggeration on the part of the children, their responses suggest a degree of physical and psychological abuse in many cases. Domestic work does in some cases acquire the characteristics of the worst forms of child labour.

Some children are even worse off. We asked the children if they knew of other working children who are being badly treated. Several children made generalised responses, which are likely to be based largely on hearsay, about children being worked excessively hard, being denied wages, being beaten, not being allowed out to meet others, and even being raped. We had eleven more specific responses, one of which turned out to be one of the unhappy children in our sample. These are the children's observations.

A girl in Kwekwe knew of another girl:

> She is 17. Her work is vending. She gets up at five to fetch water to wash and to do all the housework. When she is finished, she goes to the market to buy goods and then starts selling them where she is in the sun, even in the middle of the day.

A boy in Mabvuku (Harare) knew of a girl who had to do all the housework and the work in the garden and was not allowed to meet people.

A boy in Kadoma knew of a young boy nearby who was not allowed out, even to go to his rural home. It appears that the boy was appren ticed to someone who dealt with traditional medicines and so was not allowed to talk to people lest he reveal the secrets of his trade.

A girl in Kadoma said some children are not allowed out of the houses where they work and gave an example of a young boy she knew:

> He wanted to return to his home in Zvimba. They refuse him food and are mean with everything. They treat him badly. He is given clothes by the people next door, who come from Botswana.

A girl in Kadoma reported of a girl she knew:

> She lives in the house and is not allowed to go outside. She told me that she is not being treated well. If anything goes wrong at the house, they say she is responsible. With her work, she gets no rest. Sometimes she does not sleep. When the employers go to bed, they can give her more chores that she must do. If they find these not done when they get up, they beat her.

Another boy in Kadoma told us of a girl he knew:

> ... They give her work that she is not supposed to do, like hoeing in the garden or arranging flowers, while she is supposed only to look after the house. They beat her and pay her late... Those people know that they work her like a donkey.

A girl in Kadoma knew of another girl:

> They beat her and are mean with food and the money she works for. She is always crying, which is pitiful. She wants to return to her home in Mhondoro, but when she says she wants to go, they keep her money.

A boy in Zvishavane told us of the boy next door:

> There lives another boy who is made to work without being given his money. Sometimes if he makes a mistake over something little, they deduct his money as if he were a prostitute... He has no parents. He does not go to school. Where he lives, he is beaten and given little food if he makes a mistake. The woman he works for is his father's sister. He is 14 years old.

Another boy in Zvishavane reported:

> There is a friend... He is breathing fire like me, working for his mbuya.[110] He is 13 years old, and is not going to school. He lives with his father, who is sick and cannot do anything

for himself. He wants to stop working, but he is forced to go on working. The money he is given is small and he is given only part of his pay.

A boy in Chinhoyi knows of a girl who works for little money. She has no days off and is not allowed out of the house at any time.

A girl in Chitungwiza, herself happy in her work, knew of two who were working for very small money.

In workshops attended by child domestic workers, children mention sexual abuse as being a common problem for domestic workers. None of the children in the initial survey mentioned such abuse as happening to them, but abused children would be unlikely to bring the matter up in the context of a semi-formal interview, or in a written response to a questionnaire. One girl did speak openly about being raped.

Vongai was a 17-year-old girl, one of six children, whose parents divorced when she was twelve years old. Her father remarried and Vongai's stepmother was not willing to look after so many children. Their father left his children from his first marriage at his newly acquired rural plot, where there was only one pole-and-mud hut. There was very little food and no money, the children decided to move in with their mother who had remained at the matrimonial home.

The mother told her children that as she was not working she could not afford to send them to school. She sent the older girls, Vongai and her sister, to her young sister living in the small town of Zvishavane, who in turn found Vongai employment with a couple in her church.

Where Vongai worked first as a housemaid, her duties included cleaning, washing, sweeping, scrubbing, ironing, cooking, and helping with goods for trade. The family had four children, including a girl and a boy older than Vongai, who never helped with household chores. The parents were often away on business. Vongai said she used to wake up around five in the morning and went to bed no earlier than nine in the evening. She was off duty only once in the three months she worked there. Food was readily available; she used to eat what everyone ate. The only problem was that she did not have enough time to sit down and eat. Sometimes she was assigned duties when she was about to sit down for her meals or when she was eating. She slept on the floor of the bedroom of the eldest daughter of the house, who slept in a bed.

> My relatives were not allowed to visit as they said they were disturbing me to do my work. If they did come I would be taken to task explaining what they wanted. They would even ask what they had taken. They thought allrelatives of maids came to steal and I would talk to them outside the gate.

While Vongai got along well with the girl, the boy did not like the new maid, accusing her of not ironing his clothes well, forbidding her from sitting on the sofas, and accusing her of trying to seduce his father.

Once, when the parents were away, the boy raped her. She reported the matter to her aunt, told a friend of the boy and the daughter of the house, who in turn informed the parents when they returned. She was sent back to her mother's rural home while the case was being discussed. When her mother threatened to expose the case, it was agreed that Vongai should work for her employer's sister. The families tried to settle the matter to avoid a scandal, with Vongai's parents demanding considerable payments in damages.

Eventually, encouraged by members of the local club for child domestic workers, Vongai reported the matter to the ZDAWU officer, and charges were pressed. Her new employer was unhappy with visits from the police and further pressure was applied to get the girl to marry the boy who had raped her.

Vongai was thankful to the union for bringing the case into the open and helping her to avoid an unwanted marriage, commenting,

> I am sure that there are more children with cases similar to mine or even worse. Some are given AIDS by their employers and these are not reported, some work as sex workers with adults collecting the money.
>
> Children are being treated as slaves in the households and no one ever sees or cares.

Vongai received consolation in the club for child domestic workers, where she found friends with similar backgrounds, sympathy, and moral support. The club members who knew about Vongai's case urged her to press charges, as they said her case should set a precedent in their area.[111]

Here we see children in the club wanting the case to be brought to court to make it clear that child employees could not be abused at will. In discussions, child domestic workers have complained that when they report abuse, they often receive little sympathy or help from authorities. Sometimes the authorities even add to the abuse. If they do respond, the process of taking up a case is slow, and the children believe that denial by adults is likely to be accepted in the face of accusations by children.

In these stories, apart from sexual abuse, we find examples of compulsion to work and lack of freedom to leave; excessive working hours; physical abuse; psychological abuse; and isolation from family and friends – all characteristics that place the work among the worst forms of child labour. Such treatment of children cannot be accepted in our society.

Recommendations

• Children need to be informed of support services such as Childline.[112]

• Parents and guardians should ensure that when their children are away at work, someone trustworthy regularly checks that they are being treated well.

• Children's complaints about abuse should be listened to and investigated and where appropriate these should be brought into the open, to make clear what is not to be tolerated.

NOTES

110. The term covers various relationships such as grandmother or mother's brother's wife.

111. We later heard that she had given in to family pressure, dropped charges and opted for marriage.

112. Childline is an organisation concerned about child abuse, and offering free-phone (961 in Zimbabwe) and free-post (Box CY1400, Harare; Box 1795, Bulawayo) services to children, as well as a drop-in centre in Harare.

9

Clubs for Child Domestic Workers

Officers of ZDAWU have been helping child domestic workers to form clubs so that they can meet regularly with other children in a similar position to theirs. The meetings have a social and recreational function, as well as an educational one. The clubs have joined other clubs of working children, sending representatives to meetings of a national organisation for working children, which is in turn affiliated to the African Movement of Working Children and Youth. The clubs provide the children with an opportunity to talk about their situation and to consider with others how to deal with problems they face. The organisation encourages the children to speak out, with some hope of being heard by people who can influence their lives. They report regularly on progress made in having their rights respected. In some countries, members of the Movement have been able to meet with government officials and influence policy.[113] Apart from any influence they may have, the chance to speak out and to be heard has the effect of raising the children's self-esteem.[114] It allows some of them to break out of an attitude of passive acceptance of their situation and to work to improve it.

In the clubs, the children encourage other members to speak out about the way they are treated. We saw them encouraging a member to press charges for rape. On other occasions, they have denounced the practice of children pretending that they are members of the family rather than workers, in order to save their employers from attention.

Apart from teaching children about their rights as employees and as children, it is planned that the clubs will also take on an educational and training role. The groups are following the example of clubs for child domestic workers in Senegal and other countries in West Africa, which have grown into a broad movement of working children. This movement has been able to negotiate help for the children, particularly in the areas of education and training, and of better working conditions. Sometimes they have helped children in particularly stressful employment to find alternative forms of income.

Particularly in Zvishavane, the children are involved in active drama groups, which enable them to express their problems to the public. These groups have support from the local communities and the children are enthusiastic about the help they have received.

> Another message I want to convey is to thank the children of ZDAWU and Mr Chikozho [the facilitating officer] for helping other children in Zvishavane.

A boy in Masvingo has learned some lessons that he wishes to pass on to other working children.

> I want to say some things to be known by other children who work in the house. That is, if you are not given your money, you should go to ZDAWU and report your case. If you are not satisfied with the work you do, you can stop that job. If you want another job, you can go to ZDAWU, who will look for a good job.

> You must know that your work should not spoil your health. Do not keep forcing yourself to spoil your life. You who work, if you see that working brings money together with trouble, you must take care of yourself and not forget the trouble. You must not use the money to get drunk, because there is a virus that kills [referring to HIV, spread by casual sex that goes with drinking].

It is, however, sometimes difficult for children to join the activities of the clubs. Child workers are not always able to get time off for the meetings. When they have very limited time off, there may be other things they want to do. If they do not live very near the meeting place, it is difficult for them to meet transport costs to attend the meetings.

In some towns, it is difficult to find appropriate venues. The open is unpleasant in wet weather. Some groups have been meeting at ZDAWU offices, but these are not conducive for recreational activities. Sometimes the venues they find are open to public interference.

The children need support in running their clubs. ZDAWU officers have other work to do and do not always have sufficient time to give the clubs the help they need. Where the clubs are most successful, they receive support from local communities and local business. For example, in Zvishavane, the children's club was given a piece of land by the mine to start market gardening, while the members of the local miners wives' club were willing and prepared to teach the children how to grow vegetables.

One of the common desires of children in ZDAWU is for education and training. In 2005, part-time teachers were employed to provide basic education in the clubs. This is likely to fulfil a further need for many of the children.

Another common request from children is help in developing income-generating activities – in other words activities that will give them a little extra money. However, since the children already have considerable workloads, it would be more appropriate to ensure that they are properly paid for the work they do. Another reason for income-generating activities is the hope that such an alternative income will eventually enable them to become independent of domestic work. Unfortunately, in a collapsing economy there is strong competition for any niche that might generate income and it is difficult to find activities outside employment that will create adequate income for the children.

Recommendations

• These clubs can be beneficial to children socially, educationally, and in other ways and should be encouraged.

• Employers should ensure that the children in their charge are able to attend the meetings of their nearest club.

• Local communities should provide support, providing facilities, guidance where necessary, and other forms of help.

• The children in the clubs should be encouraged to identify and help those children with special needs.

• These clubs should be given greater publicity through invitations to address public functions and celebrations (such as Workers' Day) so that the causes they are fighting for are heard by the whole nation.

NOTES

113. See the reports on activities at http://www.enda.sn/eja

114. See Jacquemin, 'Children's domestic work in Abidjan...', p. 395.

10

Conclusion

Save the Children's policy on children and work emphasises that we should be guided by the best interests of children, that we should see the benefits of work to the children, and that it is often preferable to improve the conditions of working children, rather than to remove them from their source of livelihood. Sometimes, however, children are in a working situation so harmful to them that we should be looking to remove them from it. Here we are to be guided by the ILO Convention 182 on the worst forms of child labour and its accompanying recommendation, 190.

We have seen that some of the conditions of some child domestic workers do meet the criteria laid out in these documents. Children are sometimes forced to work. Their hours are sometimes excessive. The pay is sometimes inadequate. Some of their tasks are hazardous. Their education is neglected. They are restricted from returning home and from meeting with their peers. While we do not have exact numbers, we have evidence that urgent redress is required for a significant number of children. We suggest that the children themselves are best able to identify those in such circumstances and they can then seek redress with the help of the supporting trade union, who in turn can call upon other appropriate agencies.

UNICEF has warned of the problematic nature of child domestic work in general. There is a danger that distinguishing the worst employers from the rest will result in ignoring the problems that children always face in this kind of work.[115] Indeed, we would prefer a world in which no children needed this kind of employment for their livelihood. The children, however, clearly distinguish employers who care for them, often as members of the employers' family, from others who treat them badly. They see benefits in their employment when they are treated well.[116]

The majority of children do not want to be removed from employment and we should take seriously their perceptions of what is in their best interests. In most cases we do well to follow the policy of Save the Children in trying to discern both positive and negative elements of children's work, in order to improve the children's situation. In spite of the many problems that domestic employment brings to children, to abolish the employment of children will not benefit those children who need money. While in other countries it is feasible to remove children from employment and back into school by providing their families with an alternative income,[117] this is unlikely to be feasible for the majority of working children in Zimbabwe, since resources are not available to provide such income in the present economic climate and in any case many of the children do not have families to support them. Here a more realistic policy is to capitalise on the benefits that employment can bring to children. As long as we are unable to offer the children something better, we should commend rather than condemn employers who offer their young employees a chance to improve their lives and take care of their well-being and futures.

Accordingly, we are not against rewarding children with payment for their work. We are, however, in favour of providing working children with an environment that respects their dignity and gives them an opportunity to develop. We respect the wishes of the children to have their conditions of work improved.

We have pointed out that the employment of children is not the same as the employment of adults. We have made recommendations that we would not make for adult employees. We recommended that the child's family ensure regular visits to the working child; that employers ensure that children are able to visit their families regularly; that they have adequate time for sleep. We acknowledge that employers are responsible for the well-being and safety of the children, which limits the children's freedom to go where they please. We have also recommended that employers be responsible for the child's continuing education, as an element of the child's well-being.

We have noticed that children are happier when they are to some extent incorporated into the employer's family. It helps when the employer is related or at least known to the child's family. It helps when the child eats with the family, and can play with the children of the family. All this fits the image of child domestic workers as poor children who have been brought into a wealthier family for their own benefit. The employer is a patron to the child.

On the other hand, we have also seen that children with formal contracts are more likely to be content than the majority who have none. The image of child domestic workers being drawn into their patron's families, means that there is no clear demarcation of duties for which the child is to paid. The hours of work are not defined. There is no clear allocation of days off or leave. Work can expand indefinitely. We have seen cases of children being unhappily exploited even by relatives.

So both child and employer must find a balance between the formal employment of an adult and informal patronage for children who need care and support.

Critical in the treatment of child domestic workers are attitudes to children and attitudes to poverty. One of the problems facing the poor in post-colonial Zimbabwean society is that as people have moved into the wealthier classes, some have adopted the ways of the colonial, racially-based class structure. In particular, employees are kept at a distance, away from the facilities enjoyed by the employer's family, and are expected to do whatever is asked (such as washing underwear) irrespective of cultural values.

In contrast, we propose that in a healthy society, poor people are treated with respect, and accorded the rights due to any people. Poor children who work hard to improve their situation deserve particular respect and appreciation. This would help to restore their self confidence and self esteem, which is often damaged in the face of the hardships they face.

NOTES

115. *Child Domestic Work*, pp. 14–15.

116. In this respect, the opinions of child domestic workers differ from, for example, child workers in Nepal, who consider that conditions for domestic workers are universally so bad that child domestic work in their country should be considered one of the 'worst forms' of child labour. See Maggie Black, *Child Domestic Workers: Finding a Voice* (London, Anti-Slavery International, 2002), p. 54.

117. See L. Groves, *Good Practice in working children's participation: A Case Study from Brazil* (Report to International Save the Children Alliance, 2003).

Appendix 1
Tables

Table 1: The sample by town

		Frequency	Percent
Valid	Harare Mabvuku-Tafara	3	2
	Harare Chitungwiza	23	16
	Harare Mufakose	4	3
	Harare Dzivaresekwa	11	8
	Chinhoyi	26	18
	Kadoma	6	4
	Kwekwe	3	2
	Gweru	8	6
	Zvishavane Maglass	25	18
	Zvishavane Mandava	8	6
	Masvingo	23	16
	Bulawayo	3	2
	Total	143	99
Missing	Unknown	1	1
Total		144	100

Table 2: Age and Gender

		Gender		Total
		boy	girl	
Age	under 12	1	2	3
	12-14	16	19	35
	15-17	30	68	98
	18	2	4	6
Total		49	93	142

Table 3: Happy with work, by age

		Are you happy in your work?			Total
		yes	no	partly	
Age	Under 12	1		1	2
	12-14	25	8		33
	15-17	35	48	4	87
	18	3	3		6
Total		64	59	5	128

Missing cases 16   Probability according to Pearson chi-square: .004

Table 4: Happy with work, by gender

		Are you happy in your work?			Total
		yes	no	partly	
Gender	boy	28	15	3	46
	girl	38	44	2	84
Total		66	59	5	130

Missing cases 14   Probability according to Pearson chi-square: .007

Table 5: Wanting to stop

		Are you happy in your work?			Total
		yes	no	partly	
Do you want to stop working?	yes	18	27		45
	no	47	29	5	81
Total		65	56	5	125

Missing cases 19   Probability according to Pearson chi-square: .007

Table 6: With whom were you living before you started working?

		Frequency	Percent
Valid	Both parents	52	36
	Mother only	49	34
	Father only	11	8
	Relative	21	15
	Other Adult	8	6
	Other	1	1
Missing	No response	2	1
	Total	144	101

Table 7: Did you wish to work?

		Are you happy in your work?			Total
		yes	no	partly	
Did you want to work?	yes	56	38	3	97
	no	10	21	2	33
Total		66	59	5	130

Missing cases 14   Probability according to Pearson chi-square: .022

Table 1: The sample by town

		Frequency	Percent
Valid	Harare Mabvuku-Tafara	3	2
	Harare Chitungwiza	23	16
	Harare Mufakose	4	3
	Harare Dzivaresekwa	11	8
	Chinhoyi	26	18
	Kadoma	6	4
	Kwekwe	3	2
	Gweru	8	6
	Zvishavane Maglass	25	18
	Zvishavane Mandava	8	6

Table 9: Relations between the employer and the child's family

		Are you happy in your work?			Total
		yes	No	partly	
Family relations with employer	Related	10	5		15
	Known but not related	27	13		40
	Not previously known	29	41	5	75
	Total	66	59	5	130

Missing cases 14   Probability according to Pearson chi-square: .007

Table 10: Distance between place of work and previous home

		Frequency	Percent
Valid	0-5 km	49	34
	6-20 km	8	6
	21-50 km	13	9
	51-100 km	22	15
	over 100 km	52	36
	Total	144	100

Table 11: Effects of distance

		Are you happy in your work?		Total
		yes	No/partly	
Distance from previous home	0-5 km	26	19	45
	Over 5 km	40	45	85
	Total	66	64	130

Missing cases 14   Probability according to Pearson chi-square: .24

Table 12: Visits by relatives

| | | Are you happy in your work? | | | Total |
		yes	no	partly	
Do relatives visit you?	yes	39	23	1	63
	no	25	34	4	63
Total		64	57	5	128

Missing cases 18   Probability according to Pearson chi-square: .028

Table 13: Contracts

| | | Are you happy in your work? | | | Total |
		yes	no	partly	
Do you have a formal contract?	yes	28	10	1	39
	no	36	49	3	88
Total		64	59	4	127

Missing cases 13   Probability according to Pearson chi-square: .005

Table 14: School level reached

		Frequency	Percent	Valid Percent	Cumulative Percent
Valid	None	5	4	4	100
	Some primary	28	19	21	96
	Reached grade 7	36	25	27	75
	Some secondary	57	40	43	49
	Reached Form 4	8	6	6	6
	Total	134	93	100	
Missing	No response	10	7		
Total		144	100		

It is likely that some of those who failed to respond had little or no education

Table 15: Still in school

		Frequency	Percent	Cumulative Percent
Valid	yes	37	26	26
	some other course	1	1	27
	no	104	72	100
	Total	142	99	
Missing	No response	2	1	
Total		116	100	

Table 16: Still in school by level reached

		Still in school		
		yes	No	Total
School level reached	None		5	5
	Some primary	16	12	28
	Reached grade 7	7	28	35
	Some secondary	12	45	57
	Reached Form 4	2	6	8
Total		37	96	133

Missing cases 11   Probability according to Pearson chi-square: .003

Table 17: Who pays the school fees?

		Frequency	Percent	Valid Percent	Cumulative Percent
Valid	employer	10	7	27	27
	self	10	7	27	54
	parent or relative	16	11	43	97
	other	1	1	3	100
	Total	37	26	100	
Missing	N/a	105	73		
	No response	2	1		
Total		144	100		

Table 18: Still in school by are you happy in your work

		Are you happy in your work?			Total
		yes	no	partly	
Still in school	yes	28	6	1	35
	no	38	53	4	95
Total		66	59	5	130

Missing cases 14   Probability according to Pearson chi-square: .000

Table 19: Still in school by age

| | | Still in school | | Total |
		Yes	no	
Age	under 12	1	2	3
	12-14	22	13	35
	15-17	14	82	96
	18		6	6
Total		37	103	140

Missing cases 4   Probability according to Pearson chi-square: .000

Table 20: Reasons for not being in school

		Frequency	Percent	Valid Percent
Valid	No money	83	58	90
	no time	1	1	1
	other	8	6	9
	Total	92	65	100
Missing	n/a	37	25	
	No response	15	10	
	Total	52	35	
Total		144	100	

Table 21: Hours of work

		Frequency	Percent	Valid Percent	Cumulative Percent
Valid	2 or less	1	1	1	1
	2.1-6	34	24	31	32
	6.1-8	26	18	24	56
	8.1-10	27	19	25	81
	Over 10	21	15	19	100
	Total	109	76	100	
Missing	Missing	35	24		
Total		144	100		

Descriptive statistics: Minimum recorded   2 hours
                               Maximum recorded   15 hours
                               Mean   7.6 hours

Table 22: Hours of work by still in school

| | | Still in school? | | Total |
		yes	no	
Daily hours of work	2 or less	1		1
	2.1-6	22	12	34
	6.1-8	5	20	25
	8.1-10	3	24	27
	Over 10	2	18	20
Total		33	74	107

Missing cases 37   Probability according to Pearson chi-square: .000

Table 23: Time off to rest

		Frequency	Percent
Valid	yes	75	52
	yes but very little	5	4
	no	62	432
	Total	142	99
Missing	No response	2	1
Total		144	100

Table 24: Do you have time to play with others?

		Frequency	Percent
Valid	yes	66	46
	no	72	50
	Total	138	96
Missing	No response	6	4
Total		144	100

Table 25: Days off

		Frequency	Percent
Valid	Yes	96	67
	No	44	31
	Total	140	97
Missing	No response	4	3
Total		144	100

Table 26: Leave

		Frequency	Percent
Valid	yes	65	45
	no	77	54
	Total	142	99
Missing	No response	2	1
Total		144	100

Table 27: Are you left alone with children?

		Are you left alone with children?		Total
		Yes	no	
Age	under 12	1	2	3
	12-14	14	18	32
	15-17	33	58	91
	18	2	4	6
Total		50	82	132

Missing cases 12

Table 28: Are you left alone in the house?

		Are you left alone in the house?		Total
		yes	no	
Age	under 12	1	2	3
	12-14	9	23	32
	15-17	57	33	90
	18	5	1	6
Total		72	59	131

Missing cases 13   *Probability according to Pearson chi-square: .002*

Table 29: Punishment for mistakes

		Frequency	Percent
	Scolded	66	46
	Beaten*	20	14
	Money withheld **	10	7
	Food withheld	3	2
	Advice	25	17
	None	11	8
	Total	137	95
Missing	No response	7	5
	Total	144	100

* Some of these cases explicitly mentioned scolding as well
** Includes paying for broken or lost items

Table 30: Are you happy with the way your employer treats you?

		Frequency	Percent	Valid Percent
	yes	44	31	33
Valid	no	87	60	65
	partly	3	2	2
	Total	134	93	100
Missing	No response	10	7	
	Total	144	100.0	

Table 31: Is your employer satisfied with your performance?

		Frequency	Percent	Valid Percent
	yes	59	41	43
Valid	no	54	38	40
	do not know	23	16	17
	Total	136	94	100
Missing	No response	8	6	
	Total	144	100	

Table 32: Were you taught to use equipment?

		Frequency	Percent
	yes	94	65
Valid	No	43	30
	Total	137	95
Missing	No response	7	5
Total		144	100

Table 33: Do you ever feel in danger at work?

		Frequency	Percent
	yes	55	38
Valid	no	72	50
	Total	127	88
Missing	No response	17	12
Total		144	100

Table 34: Have you ever suffered an accident at work?

		Frequency	Percent
	yes	31	22
Valid	no	108	75
	Total	139	97
Missing	No response	5	3
Total		144	100

Table 35: Where do you live?

		Frequency	Percent
	with employer	95	66
	with parents/guardians	34	24
Valid	other	14	10
	Not known	1	1
	Total	144	100

Table 36: Where do you sleep? (applicable only to those staying with employer)

		Frequency	Percent
Valid	outhouse	4	4
	kitchen/dining/living area	40	43
	bedroom	48	52
	Total	92	99
Missing	n/a	45	
	No response	7	
	Total	52	
Total		144	

Table 37: Do you eat with the family for whom you work?

		Frequency	Percent
Valid	yes	55	43
	same food eaten separately	32	25
	different food, eaten separately	40	31
	Total	127	99
Missing	n/a	17	
Total		144	

Table 38: Eating arrangements by happy in work

		Are you happy in your work?			Total
		yes	no	partly	
Do you eat with the family?	yes	45	6	2	53
	same food eaten separately	18	9	1	28
	different food, eaten separately	3	34	1	38
Total		66	49	4	119

Missing cases 25   Probability according to Pearson chi-square: .000

110

Table 39: Have been sick at work?

		Frequency	Percent
Valid	Yes	52	36
	No	88	61
	Total	140	97
Missing	No response	4	4
Total		144	100

Table 40: Who looked after you while you were sick?

		Frequency	Percent	Valid Percent
Valid	employer	16	11	31
	relative	17	12	33
	other	3	2	6
	No one	16	11	31
	Total	52	36	100
Missing	n/a	91	63	
	No response	1	1	
	Total	92	64	
Total		144	100	

Table 41: Are you happy with the way the employer's family treats you?

		Frequency	Percent	Valid Percent
Valid	yes	61	42	46
	no	69	48	52
	partly	2	1	2
	Total	132	92	100
Missing	No response	12	8	
Total		144	100	

111

Appendix 2: Guidelines for employers of child domestic workers

(as circulated by ZDAWU)

1. Recruiting Child Domestic Workers

1.1. Both the child and the guardians must be willing partners and agree to the arrangement.

1.2. A formal contract should be drawn up, indicating responsibilities, hours of work, holidays and other benefits, terms of payment, and any other agreements relevant to the employment (a suitable form of contract can be obtained from ZDAWU officers).

1.3. The contract should state what provisions are being made for the child's continued education or training, and the responsibility of the employer in this respect.

1.4. When the child is living far from home, employers should ensure that he or she has adequate opportunity to visit their family regularly.

1.5. Guardians should ensure that a relative, or someone trusted by the child, visits the child regularly at the place of work, to ensure that the child is happy and being treated well, and to provide contact with the family.

2. Conditions of Work

2.1. Children must be treated with respect. Even when correction is needed, this should be done in a way that does not remove the human dignity of the child (shouting at the child or beating the child is not appropriate).

2.2. Young children should be given clear encouragement when they work well.

2.3. The hours of work should be moderate and relate to the age of children, their need for time for schooling, and the pay they receive. The law requires that no child be required to work more than 6 hours a day, or for more than 3 hours continuously without a break of at least 15 minutes.

2.4. Wages should be related to inflation, and ensure that the children can buy what they need, with something to spare for their families or to save.

2.5. The work and responsibilities given to the children should be appropriate for their ages. In particular, children have raised the following issues:

> a. Young children under 13 can be expected to do only simple tasks like sweeping and washing dishes. They should not be expected to do the laundry of the whole household. They should not be left alone with younger children, although they can play with toddlers when there is an adult around.
>
> b. Children under 15 should not work with poisonous chemicals.
>
> c. Children under 15 should not be required to do heavy gardening work
>
> d. Children under 15 should not be expected to handle money in an employer's business.
>
> e. Children under 15 should not be left alone in the house, and should not be left alone in charge of younger children.
>
> f. Children under 18 should not be left alone in the house overnight.
>
> g. Children under 18 should not be left to care for babies for more than half a day.
>
> h. Children under 18 should not be sent out at night.

2.6. Cultural values of the children should be respected.

2.7. The children should be carefully instructed on safety procedures with respect to any equipment they use (particularly respecting electricity).

2.8. Children should be provided with appropriate protective clothing when liable to come into contact with harmful substances, such as chemicals or refuse.

2.9. Children should not be sent out at times and to places that may be dangerous, particularly at night.

2.10. Children should receive compensation for injuries arising out of their work.

2.11. Children should get regular days off work, which should be fully respected both at their place of work and in their homes. The law requires 1 1/2 days off per week, of which 24 hours must be continuous.

Children complain that after working all week in their employers' homes, when they go home on their day off, they are not allowed to rest but are required to do further domestic work.

3. Living Conditions

3.1. Children who live at their place of work should be provided with adequate accommodation, ensuring adequate sleep. (If they have to sleep in living spaces such as living rooms or kitchen, they should still have adequate uninterrupted sleep.)

3.2. Children should get enough time to sleep: employers of live-in working children act as their guardians (in loco parentis) and are responsible to see that they have the hours of rest appropriate to their age (8 hours for children aged 15 and above, and 9 hours for children below 15).

3.3. Children should receive enough food while at work: employers are responsible to see that this is the case if the child is living at the place of work.

3.4. When a child is living at the place of work, employers are responsible to see that he or she receives care when they are sick. Medical insurance is recommended, without which the employer should cover the costs of necessary medicines.

3.5. Children living away from home can be very lonely. In such cases, employers should ensure that the children enjoy social life with their peers.

3.6. All employers should ensure that the child worker is treated with respect by all members of the household.

4. Child Abuse

Children living away from home are open to physical, sexual and psychological abuse, and need protection.

4.1. Children need to be informed of support services such as Childline

4.2. Parents or guardians should ensure the child is visited regularly (see point 1.5 above).

5. Clubs for Child Domestic Workers

(These have been established in some centres. They help children to support each other and to enjoy a social life as well as receive appropriate informal education and training.)

5.1. Employers should ensure that the children in their charge are able to attend meetings of their nearest club.

5.2. Local communities should provide support, providing facilities, guidance, and whatever help is needed.

5.3. Where no clubs are available, employers should ensure that children have regular opportunity to mix with their peers.

www.ingramcontent.com/pod-product-compliance
Lightning Source LLC
Chambersburg PA
CBHW021834020426
42334CB00014B/621